THREE BOOKS

Ted Hughes was born in 1930. He is the author of numerous collections of poems and books for children. In 1984 he was appointed Poet Laureate.

TED HUGHES   Three Books

Remains of Elmet, Cave Birds, River

faber and faber

This edition first published in 1993
by Faber and Faber Limited
3 Queen Square London WC1N 3AU

Photoset by Wilmaset Ltd, Wirral
Printed in England by Clays Ltd, St Ives Plc

A CIP record for this book
is available from the British Library
ISBN 0–571–14082–3

10 9 8 7 6 5 4 3 2 1

Contents

CAVE BIRDS

CONTENTS

REMAINS OF ELMET

In memory of my mother and father

The Dark River

Six years into her posthumous life
My uncle raises my mother's face. He says
Yes, he would love a cup of tea.

Her memory still intact, still good
Under his baldness.
Her hands a little plumper, trembling more
Chatter his cup in its saucer.

Keeping their last eighty years alive and attached to me.
Keeping their strange depths alive and attached to me.

And now he restores his prime
Exercising everything that happened,
As his body tries to renew its cells —

Empty air, hijacked in the larynx
To fly a dream, populated with glimpses —

And the smoky valley never closes,
The womb that bore him, chimney behind chimney,
Horizons herded — behind encircling horizons,
A happy hell, the arguing, immortal dead,
The hymns rising past farms.

So he has brought me my last inheritance:
Archaeology of the mouth: the home fire's embers,
Fluff, breath-frail, from under the looms of Egypt.
Funeral treasures that crumble at the touch of day —

The huge fish, the prize of a lifetime,
Exhausted at the surface, the eye staring up at me,
But on such a frayed, fraying hair-fineness –

Any moment now, a last kick –
And the dark river will fold it away.

Abel Cross, Crimsworth Dene

Where the Mothers
Gallop their souls

Where the howlings of heaven
Pour down on to earth
Looking for bodies
Of birds, animals, people

A happiness starts up, secret and wild,
Like a lark-song just out of hearing
Hidden in the wind

A silent evil joy
Like a star-broken stone
Who knows nothing more can happen to it
In its cradle-grave.

Football at Slack

Between plunging valleys, on a bareback of hill
Men in bunting colours
Bounced, and their blown ball bounced.

The blown ball jumped, and the merry-coloured men
Spouted like water to head it.
The ball blew away downwind —

The rubbery men bounced after it.
The ball jumped up and out and hung on the wind
Over a gulf of treetops.
Then they all shouted together, and the ball blew back.

Winds from fiery holes in heaven
Piled the hills darkening around them
To awe them. The glare light
Mixed its mad oils and threw glooms.
Then the rain lowered a steel press.

Hair plastered, they all just trod water
To puddle glitter. And their shouts bobbed up
Coming fine and thin, washed and happy

While the humped world sank foundering
And the valleys blued unthinkable
Under depth of Atlantic depression —

But the wingers leapt, they bicycled in air
And the goalie flew horizontal

And once again a golden holocaust
Lifted the cloud's edge, to watch them.

Stanbury Moor

These grasses of light
Which think they are alone in the world

These stones of darkness
Which have a world to themselves

This water of light and darkness
Which hardly savours Creation

And this wind
Which has enough just to exist

Are not

A poor family huddled at a poor gleam

Or words in any phrase

Or wolf-beings in a hungry waiting

Or neighbours in a constellation

They are
The armour of bric-à-brac
To which your soul's caddis
Clings with all its courage.

First, Mills

               and steep wet cobbles
Then cenotaphs.

First, football pitches, crown greens
Then the bottomless wound of the railway station
That bled this valley to death.

The fatal wound. And faces whitening
At the windows. Even the hair whitened

The whole land was quietly drained.
Everything became very quiet.

Then the hills were requisitioned
For gravemounds.

The towns and the villages were sacked.

Everything fell wetly to bits
In the memory
And along the sides of the streets.

Over this trench
A sky like an empty helmet
With a hole in it.

And now – two minutes silence
In the childhood of earth.

Hill-Stone was Content

To be cut, to be carted
And fixed in its new place.

It let itself be conscripted
Into mills. And it stayed in position
Defending this slavery against all.

It forgot its wild roots
Its earth-song
In cement and the drum-song of looms.

And inside the mills mankind
With bodies that came and went
Stayed in position, fixed, like the stones
Trembling in the song of the looms.

And they too became four-cornered, stony

In their long, darkening, dwindling stand
Against the guerrilla patience
Of the soft hill-water.

The Weasels We Smoked out of the Bank

Ran along the rowan branch, a whole family,
Furious with ill-contained lightning
Over the ferny falls of clattering coolant.

After the time-long Creation
Of this hill-sculpture, this prone, horizon-long
Limb-jumble of near-female

The wild gentle god of everywhereness
Worships her, in a lark-rapture silence.

But the demons who did all the labouring
Run in and out of her holes

Crackling with redundant energy.

Leaf Mould

In Hardcastle Crags, that echoey museum,
Where she dug leaf mould for her handfuls of garden
And taught you to walk, others are making poems.

Between finger and thumb roll a pine-needle.
Feel the chamfer, feel how they threaded
The sewing machines.
                        And
Billy Holt invented a new shuttle
As like an ant's egg, with its folded worker,
As every other.
You might see an ant carrying one.
                        And
The cordite conscripts tramped away. But the cenotaphs
Of all the shells that got their heads blown off
And their insides blown out
Are these beech-bole stalwarts.
                        And oak, birch,
Holly, sycamore, pine.
                        The lightest air-stir
Released their love-whispers when she walked
The needles weeping, singing, dedicating
Your spectre-double, still in her womb,
To this temple of her *Missa Solemnis*.

White-faced, brain-washed by her nostalgias,
You were her step-up transformer.
She grieved for her girlhood and the fallen.
You mourned for Paradise and its fable.

Giving you the kiss of life
She hung round your neck her whole valley
Like David's harp.
Now, whenever you touch it, God listens
Only for her voice.

Leaf mould. Blood-warm. Fibres crumbled alive
Between thumb and finger.
Feel again
The clogs twanging your footsoles, on the street's steepness,
As you escaped.

Heptonstall

         — old man
Of the hills, propped out for air
On his wet bench —
Lets his memories leak.

He no longer calls the time of day
Across to Stoodley, soured on that opposite ridge.
And Stoodley has turned his back
On the museum silence.

He ignores Blackstone Edge —
A huddle of wet stones and damp smokes
Decrepit under sunsets.

He no longer asks
Whether Pecket under the East Wind
Is still living.

He raises no hand
Towards Hathershelf. He knows
The day has passed
For reunion with ancestors.

He knows
Midgley will never return.

The mantel clock ticks in the lonely parlour
On the Heights Road, where the face
Blue with arthritic stasis
And heart good for nothing now
Lies deep in the chair-back, angled
From the window-skylines,
Letting time moan its amnesia
Through telegraph wires

As the fragments
Of the broken circle of the hills
Drift apart.

Two Photographs of Top Withens

The house is ruinous enough, in my snapshot.
But most of the roofslabs are in place.
You sit holding your smile, in one of the sycamores.

We'd climbed from Stanbury.
And through all the leaves of the fierce book
To touch Wuthering Heights – a fouled nest.

My uncle wrinkles his nose
At something distasteful.
Emily's dream has flown.

But you smile in the branches – still in your twenties,
Ear cocked for the great cries.
'We could buy this place and renovate it!'

Except, of course, except,
On second thoughts, maybe, except
For the empty horror of the moor –

Mad heather and grass tugged by the mad
And empty wind
That has petrified or got rid of

Everything but the stones.
The stones are safe, being stone.
Even the spirit of the place, like Emily's,

Hidden beneath stone.
Nothing's left for sightseers – only a book.
It was a blue day, with larks, when I aimed my camera.

We had all the time in the world.
Walt would live as long as you had lived.
Then the timeless eye blinked.
                              And weatherproofed,
Squared with Water Authority concrete, a roofless
Pissoir for sheep and tourists marks the site
Of my uncle's disgust.
                      But the tree –
That's still there, unchanged beside its partner,
Where my camera caught (for a moment) a ghost.

Wild Rock

                Tamed rock.
Millstone-grit – a soul-grinding sandstone.

Roof-of-the-world-ridge wind
And rain, and rain.

Heaven – the face of a quarry.
Oak-leaves of hammered copper, as in Cranach.
Grass greening on acid.

Wind. Cold. A permanent weight
To be braced under. And rain.

A people fixed
Staring at fleeces, blown like blown flames.

A people converting their stony ideas
To woollen weave, thick worsted, dense fustians

Between their bones and the four trembling quarters.

Moors

Are a stage
For the performance of heaven.
Any audience is incidental.

A chess-world of top-heavy Kings and Queens
Circling in stilted majesty
Tremble the bog-cotton
Under the sweep of their robes.

Fools in sunny motley tumble across,
A laughter – fading in full view
To grass-tips tapping at stones.

The witch-brew boiling in the sky-vat
Spins electrical terrors
In the eyes of sheep.

Fleeing wraith-lovers twist and collapse
In death-pact languor
To bedew harebells
On the spoil-heaps of quarries.

Wounded champions lurch out of sunset
To gurgle their last gleams into potholes.

Shattered, bowed armies, huddling leaderless
Escape from a world
Where snipe work late.

Tick Tock Tick Tock

Peter Pan's days of pendulum
Cut at the valley groove.

Tick Tock Tick Tock
Everlasting play bled the whole unstoppable Calder
And incinerated itself happily
From a hundred mill chimneys.

Tick Tock Summer Summer
Summer Summer.
And the hills unalterable and the old women unalterable.
And the ageless boy
Among the pulsing wounds of Red Admirals.

Somebody else acted Peter Pan.
I swallowed an alarm clock
And over the school playground's macadam
Crawled from prehistory towards him
Tick Tock Tick Tock the crocodile.

There Come Days to the Hills

Of armadas about to set out —
Fresh mediaeval paintwork
Dragons on mainsails
A shouting throughout heaven

The moorlines cast off ropes, heaving their sides
Patched with harbour reflections
Turn into the light, nosing the distance
Strain in position, fluttering pennants

And the light itself leans taut
Tacking overtaking returning
Urgent and important

Everywhere exhilarated water

Even the sheep, standing windslapped
High in rigging
Look heroic

Every flashing face gazes westward —

Chinese History of Colden Water

A fallen immortal found this valley –
Leafy conch of whispers
On the shore of heaven. He brought to his ear
The mad singing in the hills,
The prophetic mouth of the rain –

These hushings lulled him. So he missed
The goblins toiling up the brook.
The clink of fairy hammers forged his slumber
To a migraine of headscarves and clatter
Of clog-irons and looms and gutter water
And clog-irons and biblical texts.

Till he woke in a terror, tore free, lay panting.
The dream streamed from him. He blinked away
The bloody matter of the Cross
And the death's-head after-image of 'Poor'.

Chapels, chimneys, roofs in the mist – scattered.

Hills with raised wings were standing on hills.
They rode the waves of light
That rocked the conch of whispers

And washed and washed at his eye.

                              Washed from his ear

All but the laughter of foxes.

Rhododendrons

Dripped a chill virulence
Into my nape –
Rubberized prison-wear of suppression!

Guarding and guarded by
The Council's black
Forbidding forbidden stones.

The policeman's protected leaf!

Detestable evergreen sterility!
Over dead acid gardens
Where blue widows, shrined in Sunday, shrank

To arthritic clockwork,
Yapped like terriers and shook sticks from doorways
Vast and black and proper as museums.

Cenotaphs and the moor-silence!
Rhododendrons and rain!
It is all one. It is over.

Evergloom of official titivation –
Uniform at the reservoir, and the chapel,
And the graveyard park,

Ugly as a brass-band in India.

Auction at Stanbury

On a hillside, part farm, part stone rubble
Shitty bony cattle disconsolate
Rotten and shattered gear

Farmers resembling the gear, the animals
Resembling the strewn walls, the shabby slopes

Shivery Pakistanis
Wind pressing the whole scene towards ice

Thin black men wrapped in bits of Bradford
Waiting for a goat to come up

Curlews in April

Hang their harps over the misty valleys

A wobbling water-call
A wet-footed god of the horizons

New moons sink into the heather
And full golden moons

Bulge over spent walls.

For Billy Holt

The longships got this far. Then
Anchored in nose and chin.

Badlands where outcast and outlaw
Fortified the hill-knowle's long outlook.

A far, veiled gaze of quietly
Homicidal appraisal.

A poverty
That cut rock lumps for words.

Requisitioned rain, then more rain,
For walls and roof.

Enfolding arms of sour hills
For company.

Blood in the veins
For amusement.

A graveyard
For homeland.

Two Trees at Top Withens

Open to huge light
Wind-shepherds
Play the reeds of desolation.

Dragged out of the furnace
They rose and staggered some way.
It was God, they knew.

Now hills bear them through visions
From emptiness to brighter emptiness
With music and with silence.

Startled people look up
With sheep's heads
Then go on eating.

Sunstruck

The freedom of Saturday afternoons
Starched to cricket dazzle, nagged at a theorem –
Shaggy valley parapets
Pending like thunder, narrowing the spin-bowler's angle.

The click, disconnected, might have escaped –
A six! And the ball slammed flat!
And the bat in flinders! The heart soaring!
And everybody jumping up and running –

Fleeing after the ball, stampeding
Through the sudden hole in Saturday – but
Already clapped into hands and the trap-shout
The ball jerked back to the stumper on its elastic.

Everything collapsed that bit deeper
Towards Monday.

Misery of the brassy sycamores!
Misery of the swans and the hard ripple!

Then again Yes Yes a wild YES –
The bat flashed round the neck in a tight coil,
The stretched shout snatching for the North Sea –
But it fell far short, even of Midgley.

And the legs running for dear life, twinkling white
In the cage of wickets
Were cornered again by the ball, pinned to the crease,
Blocked by the green and white pavilion.

Cross-eyed, mid-stump, sun-descending headache!
Brain sewn into the ball's hide
Hammering at four corners of abstraction
And caught and flung back, and caught, and again caught

To be bounced on baked earth, to be clubbed
Toward the wage-mirage sparkle of mills
Toward Lord Savile's heather
Toward the veto of the poisonous Calder

Till the eyes, glad of anything, dropped
From the bails
Into the bottom of a teacup,
To sandwich crusts for the canal cygnets.

The bowler had flogged himself to a dishclout.
And the burned batsmen returned, with changed faces,
'Like men returned from a far journey,'
Under the long glare walls of evening

To the cool sheet and the black slot of home.

When Men Got to the Summit

Light words forsook them.
They filled with heavy silence.

Houses came to support them,
But the hard, foursquare scriptures fractured
And the cracks filled with soft rheumatism.

Streets bent to the task
Of holding it all up
Bracing themselves, taking the strain
Till their vertebrae slipped.

The hills went on gently
Shaking their sieve.

Nevertheless, for some giddy moments
A television
Blinked from the wolf's lookout.

Heather

The upper millstone heaven
Grinds the heather's face hard and small.
Heather only toughens.

And out of a mica sterility
That nobody else wants
Thickens a nectar
Keen as adder venom.

A wind from the end of the sky
Buffs and curries the grizzly bear-dark pelt
Of long skylines
Browsing in innocence
Through their lasting purple aeons.

Heather is listening
Past hikers, gunshots, picnickers
For the star-drift
Of the returning ice.

No news here
But the crumbling outcrop voices
Of grouse.

A sea of bees, meanwhile, mapped by the sun.

The Sheep Went on Being Dead

Under the Heights Road, under crucified oaks
Among slovenly bracken
In the broken spine of a fallen land.

Happy work-hum of the valley mills
Stifled the shouting above looms
Which were too sunk in the pit anyway
To share the air-stir ironically
With the sheep's crumble of doll's curls and calcium.

It was a headache
To see earth such a fierce magnet
Of death. And how the sheep's baggage
Flattened and tried to scatter, getting flatter
Deepening into that power
And indrag of wet stony death.

Time sweetens
The melting corpses of farms
The hills' skulls peeled by the dragging climate –
The arthritic remains
Of what had been a single strength
Tumbled apart, forgetting each other –

The throb of the mills and the crying of lambs
Like shouting in Flanders
Muffled away
In white curls
And memorial knuckles

Under hikers' heels.

Churn-Milk Joan

A lonely stone
Afloat in the stone heavings of emptiness
Keeps telling her tale. Foxes killed her.

You take the coins out of the hollow in the top of it.
Put your own in. Foxes killed her here.
Why just here? Why not five yards that way?
A squared column, planted by careful effort.

Sun cannot ease it, though the moors grow warm.

Foxes killed her, and her milk spilled.

Or they did not. And it did not.

Farmers brought their milk this far, and cottagers
From the top of Luddenden valley left cash
In the stone's crown, probably in vinegar,
And the farmers left their change. Relic of the plague.

Churn-milk *jamb*. And Joan did not come trudging
Through the long swoon of moorland
With her sodden feet, her nipped face.
Neither snow nor foxes made her lie down
While they did whatever they wanted.

The negative of the skylines is blank.

Only a word wrenched, and the pain came,
And her mouth opened.

                 And now all of us,
Even this stone, have to be memorials
Of her futile stumbling and screams
And awful little death.

The Canal's Drowning Black

Bred wild leopards – among the pale depth fungus.
Loach. Torpid, ginger-bearded, secret
Prehistory of the canal's masonry,
With little cupid mouths.

Five inches huge!
On the slime-brink, over bridge reflections,
I teetered. Then a ringing, skull-jolt stamp
And their beards flowered sudden anemones

All down the sunken cliff. A mad-house thrill –
The stonework's tiny eyes, two feet, three feet,
Four feet down through my reflection
Watched for my next move.

Their schooldays were over.
Peeping man was no part of their knowledge.
So when a monkey god, a Martian
Tickled their underchins with his net rim

They snaked out and over the net rim easy
Back into the oligocene –
Only restrained by a mesh of kitchen curtain.
Then flopped out of their ocean-shifting aeons

Into a two-pound jam-jar
On a windowsill
Blackened with acid rain fall-out
From Manchester's rotten lung.

Next morning, Mount Zion's
Cowled, Satanic majesty behind me
I lobbed – one by one – high through the air
The stiff, pouting, failed, paled new moons

Back into their Paradise and mine.

Alcomden

Rock has not learned
Valleys are not aware
Heather and bog-cotton fit themselves
Into their snugness, vision sealed

And faces of people that appear
Moist-eyed, confronting the whole work

With cries that wince out
Just as they shape and tear clear

The whispery husk bones of faces

Are ground into fineness of light
By a weight
And shadowy violence
Of blind skylines revolving dumbly

Ignorant in ignorant air

Cock-Crows

I stood on a dark summit, among dark summits –
Tidal dawn was splitting heaven from earth,
The oyster
Opening to taste gold.

And I heard the cock-crows kindling in the valley
Under the mist –
They were sleepy,
Bubbling deep in the valley cauldron.

Then one or two tossed clear, like soft rockets
And sank back again dimming.

Then soaring harder, brighter, higher
Tearing the mist,
Bubble-glistenings flung up and bursting to light
Brightening the undercloud,
The fire-crests of the cocks – the sickle shouts,
Challenge against challenge, answer to answer,
Hooking higher,
Clambering up the sky as they melted,
Hanging smouldering from the night's fringes.

Till the whole valley brimmed with cock-crows,
A magical soft mixture boiling over,
Spilling and sparkling into other valleys

Lobbed-up horse-shoes of glow-swollen metal
From sheds in back-gardens, hen-cotes, farms
Sinking back mistily

Till the last spark died, and embers paled

And the sun climbed into its wet sack
For the day's work

While the dark rims hardened
Over the smoke of towns, from holes in earth.

Walls at Alcomden

It set out –
Splendours burst against its brow
Broke over its shoulders.
The hills heeled, meeting the blast of space.

The stone rigging was strong.
Exhilarated men
Cupped hands and shouted to each other
And grew stronger riding the first winters.

The great adventure had begun –
Even the grass
Agreed and came with them,
And crops and cattle –

No survivors.
Here is the hulk, every rib shattered.

A few crazed sheep
Pulling its weeds
On a shore of cloud.

The Long Tunnel Ceiling

Of the main-road canal bridge
Cradled black stalactite reflections.
That was the place for dark loach!

At the far end, the Moderna blanket factory
And the bushy mask of Hathershelf above it
Peered in through the cell-window.

Lorries from Bradford, baled with plump and towering
Wools and cottons met, above my head,
Lorries from Rochdale, and ground past each other
Making that cavern of air and water tremble –

Suddenly a crash!
The long gleam-ponderous watery echo shattered.

And at last it had begun!
That could only have been a brick from the ceiling!
The bridge was starting to collapse!

But the canal swallowed its scare,
The heavy mirror reglassed itself,
And the black arch gazed up at the black arch.

Till a brick
Rose through its eruption – hung massive
Then slammed back with a shock and a shattering.

An ingot!
Holy of holies! A treasure!
A trout
Nearly as long as my arm, solid
Molten pig of many a bronze loach!

There he lay — lazy — a free lord,
Ignoring me. Caressing, dismissing
The eastward easing traffic of drift,
Master of the Pennine Pass!

Found in some thin glitter among mean gritstone,
High under ferns, high up near sour heather,

Brought down on a midnight cloudburst
In a shake-up of heaven and the hills
When the streams burst with zig-zags and explosions

A seed
Of the wild god now flowering for me
Such a tigerish, dark, breathing lily
Between the tyres, under the tortured axles.

Shackleton Hill

Dead farms, dead leaves
Cling to the long
Branch of world.

Stars sway the tree
Whose roots
Tighten on an atom.

The birds, beautiful-eyed, with soft cries,
The cattle of heaven,
Visit

And vanish.

Two

Two stepped down out of the morning star.
The grouse glowed, they were stolen embers.
The dew split colour.
And a cupped hand brimmed with cock-crows.

Two came down with long shadows
Between the dawn's fingers
With the swinging bodies of hares
And snipe robbed of their jewels.

The stream spoke its oracle of unending,
The sun spread a land at their feet.

Two dropped from the woods that hung in the sky
Bringing the scorched claws of carrion crows.
And the war opened –
                                a sudden yelling
Ricocheted among huddled roof-tops.

The guide flew up from the pathway.

The other swayed.

The feather fell from his head.
The drum stopped in his hand.
The song died in his mouth.

On the Slope

Having taken her slowly by surprise
For eighty years
The hills have won, their ring is closed.

The field-walls float their pattern
Over her eye
Whether she looks outward or inward.

Nothing added, nothing taken away.
Year after year the trout in the pools
Grow heavy and vanish without ever emerging.

Foxglove and harebell neither protest nor hope
On the steep slope where she climbs.
Out of nothing she grew here simply

Also suffering to be merely flowerlike

But with the stone agony growing in her joints
And eyes dimming with losses, widening for losses.

Curlews Lift

Out of the maternal watery blue lines

Stripped of all but their cry
Some twists of near-inedible sinew

They slough off
The robes of bilberry blue
The cloud-stained bogland

They veer up and eddy away over
The stone horns

They trail a long, dangling, falling aim
Across water

Lancing their voices
Through the skin of this light

Drinking the nameless and naked
Through trembling bills.

Bridestones

Scorched-looking, unhewn – a hill-top chapel.
Actually a crown of outcrop rock –
Earth's heart-bone laid bare.

Crowding congregation of skies.
Tense congregation of hills.
You do nothing casual here.

The wedding stones
Are electrified with whispers.

And marriage is nailed down
By this slender-necked, heavy-headed
Black exclamation mark
Of rock.

And you go
With the wreath of the weather
The wreath of the horizons
The wreath of constellations
Over your shoulders.

And from now on
The sun
Can always touch your ghost
With the shadow of this finger.

From now on
The moon can always lift your skull
On to this perch, to clean it.

Mount Zion

Blackness
Was a building blocking the moon.
Its wall — my first world-direction —
Mount Zion's gravestone slab.

Above the kitchen window, that uplifted mass
Was a deadfall —
Darkening the sun of every day
Right to the eleventh hour.

Marched in under, gripped by elders
Like a jibbing calf
I knew what was coming.
The convicting holy eyes, the convulsed Moses mouthings —
Mouths that God had burnt with the breath of the desert.
They were terrified too.
A mesmerized commissariat,
They terrified me, but they terrified each other.
And Christ was only a naked bleeding worm
Who had given up the ghost.

Women bleak as Sunday rose-gardens
Or crumpling to puff-pastry, and cobwebbed with deaths.
Men in their prison-yard, at attention,
Exercising their cowed, shaven souls.
Lips stretching saliva, eyes fixed like the eyes
Of cockerels hung by the legs,
As the bottomless cry
Beat itself numb again against Wesley's foundation stone.

Alarm shouts at dusk!
A cricket had rigged up its music
In a crack of Mount Zion wall.

A cricket! The news awful, the shouts awful, at dusk —
Like the bear-alarm, at dusk, among smoky tents —
What was a cricket? How big is a cricket?

Long after I'd been smothered in bed
I could hear them
Riving at the religious stonework
With their furious chisels and screwdrivers.

What's the First Thing You Think of?

'My brother bent at his airplane, in his attic.
I crept out. I'd left a tell-tale blood-splash
On the shavings. I'd been hewing the brass
Off a cartridge case picked up in a grouse-butt.
My knife had a deer's foot. I found our cat
And hid, nursing it, under my parents' bed.
In the end, they tracked me down by the blood.'

Or: 'The Heights Road, my brother launching a glider,
Just below where an airplane crashed by the golf-links,
(Before the war, before the RAF).
And the first hawk I ever saw and knew
Flew past with a small bird in its claw.
Another small bird bounced after it, crying,
Towed through the air on an invisible string.'

Or: 'A beeswax helm, a viking prow,
Delicate, polished, silent beside some sea
Wilder than any on earth –
       – and for all his baby-bird distress at the food
       I'd tried to spoon into him, and for all the gaping
       wound of his look, his stricken, unrecognizable look,
       that could no longer recognize me –
I had to relaunch it. I relaunched it, somehow.
I imagine – out from Flamborough. Impossibly.
(So I still cannot get it afloat or light it).'

The Beacon

You claw the door. Rain
Crashes the black taut glass.

Lights in foundering valleys, in the gulf,
Splinter from their sockets.

Lights
Over conversation and telly and dishes
In graves full of eternal silence.

Lights
Of the wolf's wraith
That cannot any longer on all these hills
Find her pelt.

While the world rolls in rain
Like a stone inside surf.

Tree

A priest from a different land
Fulminated
Against heather, black stones, blown water.

Excommunicated the clouds
Damned the wind
Cast the bog pools into outer darkness
Smote the horizons
With the jawbone of emptiness

Till he ran out of breath —

In that teetering moment
Of lungs empty
When only his eye-water protected him
He saw
Heaven and earth moving.

And words left him.
Mind left him. God left him.

Bowed —
The lightning conductor
Of a maiming glimpse — the new prophet —

Under unending interrogation by wind
Tortured by huge scaldings of light
Tried to confess all but could not
Bleed a word

Stripped to his root-letter, cruciform
Contorted
Tried to tell all

Through crooking of elbows
Twitching of finger-ends.

Finally
Resigned
To be dumb.

Lets what happens to him simply happen.

The Sluttiest Sheep in England

       that never
Get their back ends docked. Who
Doctors their wormy coughs? Maggots
Bring them down in quarry dead-ends
And the fluke reigns.

They get by
On the hill subsidy. Splash-black faces
Of psychotic mashams, possessed
By their demonic agates. They clatter
Over worthless moraines, tossing
Their ancient Briton draggle-tassel sheepskins
Or pose, in the rain-smoke, like warriors –

Eyes of the first water
Stare from perfunctory near-bald
Skulls of iguana
Like eyes trapped in helmets –

This lightning-broken huddle of summits
This god-of-what-nobody-wants

Has sent what he uses for angels
To watch you.

Wadsworth Moor

Where the millstone of sky
Grinds light and shadow so purple-fine

And has ground it so long

Grinding the skin off earth
Earth bleeds her raw true darkness

A land naked now as a wound
That the sun swabs and dabs

Where the miles of agony are numbness
And harebell and heather a euphoria

Familiar

Eighty-four years dead, younger than I am,
Your hair still full red, you sip your medicine.
Your friends are the Wesleyan vicar and the Catholic priest,
One brings you flowers, one whisky. A lifted glass –

So the fungal root and pale petal
Of tuberculosis
Raised a last bloom. I imagine your breathed
'Rocked in the Cradle of the Deep' –

My dad just four. The dyer's vat pickled to ninety
Or killed quickly (even the Owl, Cragg Jack).
Near eighty, your daughter stirred my tea,
Dug up and turned over this and that

Flotsam, heirloom bits of ghost
Under your Grace Darling heaving at the oars
Among mountainous, tenebrous foam.
Now I stand right there. And large as life

You step out of Stubbing Wharfe pub
(Like my father?) I can't see your face.
I see you pause. (Like me?) I see you squint
Down at your fob. It slips from your hand. And you boot it

Along the canal bank – all the way home.
Time scramble. Now you're getting numb,
Chin-deep in the canal, clinging to grass.
Granny (she's already trotted past you)

Told at the pub you've gone, finds you, strips you,
Rubs you dry, wraps you in a blanket, sets you
By the fire. In the blink of an eye you're away –
Back in the Stubbing Wharfe – shrouded – singing –

Fading
Into such an empty negative
Even your grave's lost. You were a seed
Of the Great Hunger, fallen among stones.

Embryo, reabsorbed in the acid-sodden
Grit of the Calder crevasse. But you escaped
Granny's Andalusian blacks, the Sabbath
Toll of the valley prison.
                And I'm proof
You've come through alive.
                      You reach a hand
As I touch at your elegy. Sweep
Me and my words aside.
                Drink, deeper,
At this mirror meniscus of paper.

Heptonstall Old Church

A great bird landed here.

Its song drew men out of rock,
Living men out of bog and heather.

Its song put a light in the valleys
And harness on the long moors.

Its song brought a crystal from space
And set it in men's heads.

Then the bird died.

Its giant bones
Blackened and became a mystery.

The crystal in men's heads
Blackened and fell to pieces.

The valleys went out.
The moorland broke loose.

Crown Point Pensioners

Old faces, old roots.
Indigenous memories.
Flat caps, polished knobs
On favoured sticks

Under the blue, widening morning and the high lark.

The map of their days, like the chart of an old board-game,
Spreads crumpled below them.
Their yarning moves over it, this way and that,
Occupying the blanks.

Attuned to each other, like the strings of a harp,
They are making mesmerizing music,
Each one bowed at his dried bony profile, as at a harp.
Singers of a lost kingdom.

Moor-water toils in the valley.

An America-bound jet, on its chalky thread,
Dozes in the dusty burning dome.

Their vowels furl downwind, on air like silk.

West Laithe Cobbles

It is all
Happening to the sun.

The fallen sun
Is in the hands of water.

There are gulleys gouged in cold hills
By the sufferings of water

And gulleys
Cut in the cold fire

By the worn-out water of women
And the lost rivers of men.

Widdop

Where there was nothing
Somebody put a frightened lake.

Where there was nothing
Stony shoulders
Broadened to support it.

A wind from between the stars
Swam down to sniff at the trembling.

Trees, holding hands, eyes closed,
Acted at world.

Some heath-grass crept close, in fear.

Nothing else
Except when a gull blows through

A rip in the fabric

Out of nothingness into nothingness

Emily Brontë

The wind on Crow Hill was her darling.
His fierce, high tale in her ear was her secret.
But his kiss was fatal.

Through her dark Paradise ran
The stream she loved too well
That bit her breast.

The shaggy sodden king of that kingdom
Followed through the wall
And lay on her love-sick bed.

The curlew trod in her womb.

The stone swelled under her heart.

Her death is a baby-cry on the moor.

Heptonstall Cemetery

Wind slams across the tops.
The spray cuts upward.

You claw your way
Over a giant beating wing.

And Thomas and Walter and Edith
Are living feathers

Esther and Sylvia
Living feathers

Where all the horizons lift wings
A family of dark swans

And go beating low through storm-silver
Toward the Atlantic.

CAVE BIRDS

An Alchemical Cave Drama

To Eric Walter White

The Scream

There was the sun on the wall — my childhood's
Nursery picture. And there my gravestone
Shared my dreams, and ate and drank with me happily.

All day the hawk perfected its craftsmanship
And even through the night the miracle persisted.

Mountains lazed in their smoky camp.
Worms in the ground were doing a good job.

Flesh of bronze, stirred with a bronze thirst,
Like a newborn baby at the breast,
Slept in the sun's mercy.

And the inane weights of iron
That come suddenly crashing into people, out of nowhere,
Only made me feel brave and creaturely.

When I saw little rabbits with their heads crushed on roads
I knew I rode the wheel of the galaxy.

Calves' heads all dew-bristled with blood on counters
Grinned like masks where sun and moon danced.

And my mate with his face sewn up
Where they'd opened it to take something out
Lifted a hand —

He smiled, in half-coma,
A stone temple smile.

Then I, too, opened my mouth to praise —

But a silence wedged my gullet.

Like an obsidian dagger, dry, jag-edged,
A silent lump of volcanic glass,

The scream
Vomited itself.

The Summoner

Spectral, gigantified,
Protozoic, blood-eating.

The carapace
Of foreclosure.

The cuticle
Of final arrest.

Among crinkling of oak-leaves – an effulgence,
Occasionally glimpsed.

Shadow stark on the wall, all night long,
From the street-light. A sigh.

Evidence, rinds and empties,
That he also ate here.

Before dawn, your soul, sliding back,
Beholds his bronze image, grotesque on the bed.

You grow to recognize the identity
Of your protector.

Sooner or later –
The grip.

After the First Fright

I sat up and took stock of my options.
I argued my way out of every thought anybody could think
But not out of the stopping and starting
Catherine wheel in my belly.
The disputation went beyond me too quickly.
When I said: 'Civilization',
He began to chop off his fingers and mourn.
When I said: 'Sanity and again Sanity and above all Sanity',
He disembowelled himself with a cross-shaped cut.
I stopped trying to say anything.
But then when he began to snore in his death-struggle
The guilt came.
And when they covered his face I went cold.

The Interrogator

Small hope now for the stare-boned mule of man
Lumped on the badlands, at his concrete shadow.

This bird is the sun's keyhole.
The sun spies through her. Through her

He ransacks the camouflage of hunger.

Investigation
By grapnel.

Some angered righteous questions
Agitate her craw.

The blood-louse
Of ether.

With her prehensile goad of interrogation
Her eye on the probe

Her olfactory X-ray
She ruffles the light that chills the startled eyeball.

Later, a dripping bagful of evidence
Under her humped robe,

She sweeps back, a spread-fingered Efreet,
Into the courts of the afterlife.

She Seemed So Considerate

And everything had become so hideous
My solemn friends sat twice as solemn
My jokey friends joked and joked

But their heads were sweating decay,
Like dead things I'd left in a bag
And had forgotten to get rid of.

I bit the back of my hand
And sniffed mortification.

Then the bird came.
She said: 'Your world has died.'
It sounded dramatic.

But my potted pet fern, the one fellow spirit I still cherished,
It actually had withered.

As if Life had decided to desert me.
As if it saw more hope for itself elsewhere.

Then this winged being embraced me saying:
'Look up at the sun. I am the one creature
Who never harmed any living thing.'

I was glad to shut my eyes, and be held.
Whether dead or unborn, I did not care.

The Judge

The pondering body of the law teeters across
A web-glistening geometry.

Lolling, he receives and transmits
Cosmic equipoise.

The offal-sack of everything that is not
The Absolute on to whose throne he lowers his buttocks.

Clowning, half-imbecile,
A Nero of the unalterable.

His gluttony
Is a strange one – his leavings are guilt and sentence.

Hung with precedents as with obsolete armour
His banqueting court is as airy as any idea.

At all hours he comes wobbling out
To fatten on the appeal of those who have fouled

His tarred and starry web.

Or squats listening
To his digestion and the solar silence.

The Plaintiff

These are the wings and beak of light!

This is your moon of pain – and the wise night-bird
Your smile's shadow.

This bird
Is the life-divining bush of your desert.

The heavy-fruited, burning tree
Of your darkness.

How you have nursed her!

Her feathers are leaves, the leaves tongues,
The mouths wounds, the tongues flames

The feet
Roots

Buried in your chest, a humbling weight
That will not let you breathe.

Your heart's winged flower
Come to supplant you.

In These Fading Moments I Wanted to Say

How close I come to flame
Just watching sticky flies play

How I cry unutterable outcry
Reading the newspaper that smells of stale refuse

How I just let the excess delight
Spill out of my eyes, as I walk along

How imbecile innocent I am

So some perfect stranger's maiming
Numbs me in freezing petroleum
And lights it, and lets me char to the spine

Even the dusty dead sparrow's eye
Lifts the head off me – like a chloroform

But she was murmuring: 'Right from the start, my life
Has been a cold business of mountains and their snow
Of rivers and their mud

Yes there were always smiles and one will do a lot
To be near one's friends
But after the bye-byes, even while the door was closing, even
    while the lips still moved
The scree had not ceased to slip and trickle
The snow-melt was cutting deeper
Through its anaesthetic
The brown bulging swirls, where the snowflakes vanished into
    themselves
Had lost every reflection.'

The whole earth
Had turned in its bed
To the wall.

The Executioner

Fills up
Sun, moon, stars, he fills them up

With his hemlock —
They darken

He fills up the evening and the morning, they darken
He fills up the sea

He comes in under the blind filled-up heaven
Across the lightless filled-up face of water

He fills up the rivers he fills up the roads, like tentacles
He fills up the streams and the paths, like veins

The tap drips darkness darkness
Sticks to the soles of your feet

He fills up the mirror, he fills up the cup
He fills up your thoughts to the brims of your eyes

You just see he is filling the eyes of your friends
And now lifting your hand you touch at your eyes

Which he has completely filled up
You touch him

You have no idea what has happened
To what is no longer yours

It feels like the world
Before your eyes ever opened

The Accused

Confesses his body –
The gripful of daggers.

And confesses his skin – the bedaubed, begauded
Eagle-dancer.

His heart –
The soul-stuffed despot.

His stomach –
The corpse-eating god.

And his hard life-lust – the blind
Swan of insemination.

And his hard brain – sacred assassin.

On a flame-horned mountain-stone, in the sun's disc,
He heaps them all up, for the judgement.

So there his atoms are annealed, as in X-rays,
Of their blood-aberration –

His mudded body, lord of middens, like an ore,

To rainbowed clinker and a beatitude

First, the Doubtful Charts of Skin

Came into my hands – I set out.

After some harmless, irrelevant marvels
And much boredom at sea

Came the wrecked landfall, sharp rocks, hands and knees
Then the small and large intestine, in their wet cave.
These gave me pause.

Then came the web of veins
Where I hung so long
For the giant spider's pleasure, twitching in the darkest corner.

Finally
After the skull-hill of visions and the battle in the valley of
    screams

After the islands of women

I came to loose bones
On a heathery moor, and a roofless church.

Wild horses, with blowing tails and manes,
Standing among tombs.

And a fallen menhir, my name carved into it,
And an epitaph:
'Under this rock, he found weapons.'

The Knight

Has conquered. He has surrendered everything.

Now he kneels. He is offering up his victory.
Unlacing his steel.

In front of him are the common wild stones of the earth –

The first and last altar
On to which he lowers his spoils.

And that is right. He has conquered in earth's name.
Committing these trophies

To the small madness of roots, to the mineral stasis
And to rain.

An unearthly cry goes up.
The Universes squabble over him –

Here a bone, there a rag.
His sacrifice is perfect. He reserves nothing.

Skylines tug him apart, winds drink him,
Earth itself unravels him from beneath –

His submission is flawless.

Blueflies lift off his beauty.
Beetles and ants officiate

Pestering him with instructions.
His patience grows only more vast.

His eyes darken bolder in their vigil
As the chapel crumbles.

His spine survives its religion,
The texts moulder —

The quaint courtly language
Of wingbones and talons.

And already
Nothing remains of the warrior but his weapons

And his gaze.
Blades, shafts, unstrung bows — and the skull's beauty

Wrapped in the rags of his banner.
He is himself his banner and its rags.

As hour by hour the sun
Deepens its revelation.

Something was Happening

While I strolled
Where a leaf or two still tapped like bluetits

I met thin, webby rain
And thought: 'Ought I to turn back, or keep going?'
Her heart stopped beating, that second.

As I hung up my coat and went through into the kitchen
And peeled a flake off the turkey's hulk,
                              and stood vacantly munching
Her sister got the call from the hospital
And gasped out the screech.

In the fifteen seconds
I was scrubbing at my nails and glancing
                              up through the window
She began to burn.

Some, who had been close, walked away
Because it was beyond help now.

They did not stay to see
Her body trying to sit up, her face unrecognizable
With the effort
Of trying to be heard,
Trying to tell
How it went on getting worse and worse —

And when I saw the quince in April tufted again with emerald,
And knew – again everything had got past me
The leather of my shoes
Continued to gleam
The silence of the furniture
Registered nothing

The earth, right to its furthest rims, ignored me.

Only the snow-burned eagle-hunter
Beating himself to keep warm
And bowing towards his trap
Started singing

(Two, three, four thousand years off key).

The Gatekeeper

A reflective sphynx.
A two-headed questioner.

First, a question –
The simple fork in the road.

You seem to choose. It is a formality.
Already yourself has confessed yourself.

All those sweatings and grinnings are redundant.
The candidate is stripped.

So much fear – its weight oozes from you.
No matter, it was upholstering ease,

It was insulation
From this stranger who wails out your name

Then drops, hugging the bare ground
Where everything is too late.

Remorse, promises, a monkey chitter
Blurting from every orifice.

Your cry is like a gasp from a turned corpse
As everything comes back. And a wingspread

Thumps you with its claws. And an eagle
Is flying

To drop you into a bog or carry you to eagles.

A Flayed Crow in the Hall of Judgement

All darkness comes together, rounding an egg.
Darkness in which there is now nothing.

A blot has knocked me down. It clogs me.
A globe of blot, a drop of unbeing.

Nothingness came close and breathed on me – a frost
A shawl of annihilation curls me up like a shrimpish foetus.

I rise beyond height – I fall past falling.
I float on a nowhere
As mist-balls float, and as stars.

A condensation, a gleam simplification
Of all that pertained.
This cry alone struggles in its tissues.

Where am I going? What will come to me here?
Is this everlasting? Is it
Stoppage and the start of nothing?

Or am I under attention?
Do purposeful cares incubate me?
Am I the self of some spore

In this white of death blackness,
This yoke of afterlife?
What feathers shall I have? What is my weakness

Good for? Great fear
Rests on the thing I am, as a feather on a hand.

I shall not fight
Against whatever is allotted to me.

My soul skinned, and my soul-skin pinned out
A mat for my judges.

The Baptist

Enfolds you, as in arms, in winding waters
A swathing of balm

A mummy bandaging
Of all your body's puckering hurts

In the circulation of sea.
A whale of furtherance

Cruises through the Arctic of stone,
Bearing you blindfold and gagged

So you dissolve, in the cool wholesome salts
Like a hard-cornered grief

An iceberg of loss
Shrinking towards the equator

A seed under snow

In its armour.

Only a Little Sleep, a Little Slumber

And suddenly you
Have not a word to say for yourself.

Only a little knife, a small incision,
A snickety nick in the brain
And you drop off, like a polyp.

Only a crumb of fungus,
A pulp of mouldy tinder
And you flare, fluttering, black out like a firework.

Who are you, in the nest among the bones?
You are the shyest bird among birds.

'I am the last of my kind.'

A Green Mother

Why are you afraid?
In the house of the dead are many cradles.
The earth is a busy hive of heavens.
This is one lottery that cannot be lost.

Here is the heaven of the tree:
Angels will come to collect you.
And here are the heavens of the flowers:
These are an ever-living bliss, a pulsing, a bliss in sleep.

And here is the heaven of the worm –
A forgiving God.
Little of you will be rejected –
Which the angels of the flowers will gladly collect.

And here is the heaven of insects.
From all these you may climb
To the heavens of the birds,
                    the heavens of the beasts, and of the fish.

These are only some heavens
Not all within your choice.
There are also the heavens
Of your persuasion.
Your candle prayers have congealed an angel, a star –
A city of religions
Like a city of hotels, a holiday city.
There too I am your guide.
In none of these is the aftertaste of death
Pronounced poor. This earth is the sweetness
Of all the heavens. It is Heaven's mother.

The grave is her breast, her nipple in its dark aura.
Her milk is unending life.

                              You shall see
How tenderly she wipes her child's face clean

Of the bitumen of blood and the smoke of tears.

As I Came, I Saw a Wood

Where trees craned in dirt, clutching at the sky
Like savages photographed in the middle of a ritual
Birds danced among them and animals took part
Insects too and around their feet flowers

And time was not present none ever stopped
Or left anything old or reached any new thing
Everything moved in an excitement that seemed permanent

They were so ecstatic
I could go in among them, touch them, even break pieces off
  them
Pluck up flowers, without disturbing them in the least.
The birds simply flew wide, but were not for one moment
  distracted
From the performance of their feathers and eyes.
And the animals the same, though they avoided me
They did so with holy steps and never paused
In the glow of fur which was their absolution in sanctity

And their obedience, I could see that.

I saw I stood in a paradise of tremblings

At the crowded crossroads of all the heavens
The festival of all the religions

But a voice, a bell of cracked iron
Jarred in my skull

Summoning me to prayer

To eat flesh and drink blood.

A Riddle

Who am I?

Just as you are my father
I am your bride.

As your speech sharpened
My silence widened.

As your laughter fitted itself
My dumbness stretched its mouth wider

As you made good progress
I was torn up and dragged

As you defended yourself
I collected your blows, I was knocked backward

As you dodged
I caught in full

As you counter-attacked
I was under your feet

As you saved yourself
I was lost

And so, when you arrived empty,
I gathered up all you had and left you

Now as you abandon yourself to your death
I hold your life

Just as surely as you are my father
I shall deliver you

My firstborn
Into a changed, unchangeable world
Of wind and of sun, of rock and water
To cry.

The Scapegoat

The beautiful thing beckoned, big-haunched he loped,
Swagged with wealth, full-organed he tottered,

His sweetnesses dribbled,
His fever misted, he wanted to sob,

His cry starved watering,
Shudderings bone-juddered his hot weakness.

The frilled lizard of cavort
Ran in his wheel like a man, burned by breath.

The baboon of panoply
Jumped at the sky-rump of a greasy rainbow.

The flag of the crotch, his glistenings tapered to touch,
Furled and unfurled, in chill draughts of sun.

The comedian
Of the leap out of the body and back in again.

Gargled a mandrake oath
In a sputter of unborn spirits, a huddle of oracles.

The joker
That the confederate pack has to defer to

Gambled and lost the whole body –
An I.O.U. signed by posterity, a smear on the light.

The champion of the swoon
Lolls his bauble head, a puppet, a zombie

And the lord of immortality is a carcase of opals,
A goat of testaments, a wine-skin of riddance,

A slaking of thistles.

After There was Nothing Came a Woman

Whose face has arrived at her mirror
Via the vulture's gullet
And the droppings of the wild dog, and she remembers it
Massaging her brow with cream

Whose breasts have come about
By long toil of earthworms
After many failures, but they are here now
And she protects them with silk

Her bones
Are as they are because they cannot escape anything
They hang as if in space
The targets of every bombardment

She found her belly
In a clockwork pool, wound by the winding and unwinding sea
First it was her toy, then she found its use
She curtains it with a flowered frock
It makes her eyes shine

She looks at the grass trembling among the worn stones

Having about as much comprehension as a lamb
Who stares at everything simultaneously
With ant-like head and soldierly bearing

She had made it but only just, just —

The Guide

When everything that can fall has fallen
Something rises.
And leaving here, and evading there
And that, and this, is my headway.

Where the snow glare blinded you
I start.
Where the snow mama cuddled you warm
I fly up. I lift you.

Tumbling worlds
Open my way

And you cling.

And we go

Into the wind. The flame-wind – a red wind
And a black wind. The red wind comes
To empty you. And the black wind, the longest wind
The headwind

To scour you.

Then the non-wind, a least breath,
Fills you from easy sources.

I am the needle

Magnetic
A tremor

The searcher
The finder

His Legs Ran About

Till they seemed to trip and trap
Her legs in a single tangle

His arms lifted things, felt through dark rooms, at last with
   their hands
Caught her arms
And lay down enwoven at last at last

His chest pushed until it came against
Her breast at the end of everything

His navel fitted over her navel as closely as possible
Like a mirror face down flat on a mirror

And so when every part
Like a bull pressing towards its cows, not to be stayed
Like a calf seeking its mama
Like a desert staggerer, among his hallucinations
Finding the hoof-churned hole

Finally got what it needed, and grew still, and closed its eyes

Then such truth and greatness descended

As over a new grave, when the mourners have gone
And the stars come out
And the earth, bristling and raw, tiny and lost
Resumes its search

Rushing through the vast astonishment.

Walking Bare

What is left is just what my life bought me
The gem of myself.
A bare certainty, without confection.
Through this blowtorch light little enough

But enough.
The stones do not cease to support me.
Valleys unfold their invitations.
A progress beyond assay, breath by breath.

I rest just at my weight.
Movement is still patient with me –
Lightness beyond lightness releasing me further.

And the mountains of torment and mica
Pass me by.

Ampler skylines lift wider wings
Of simpler light.

The blood-worn cries have hardened
To moisteners for my mouth.

Hurrying worlds of voices, on other errands,
Traffic through me, ignore me.

A one gravity keeps touching me.

For I am the appointed planet
Extinct in an emptiness

But a spark in the inhalation
Of the corolla that sweeps me.

Bride and Groom Lie Hidden for Three Days

She gives him his eyes, she found them
Among some rubble, among some beetles

He gives her her skin
He just seemed to pull it down out of the air
                                             and lay it over her
She weeps with fearfulness and astonishment

She has found his hands for him,
                         and fitted them freshly at the wrists
They are amazed at themselves,
                              they go feeling all over her

He has assembled her spine,
                           he cleaned each piece carefully
And sets them in perfect order
A superhuman puzzle but he is inspired
She leans back twisting this way and that,
                          using it and laughing incredulous

Now she has brought his feet, she is connecting them
So that his whole body lights up

And he has fashioned her new hips
With all fittings complete and with newly wound coils,
                                        all shiningly oiled
He is polishing every part,
                       he himself can hardly believe it

They keep taking each other to the sun,
                                they find they can easily
To test each new thing at each new step
And now she smooths over him the plates of his skull
So that the joints are invisible

And now he connects her throat,
                        her breasts and the pit of her stomach
With a single wire

She gives him his teeth, tying their roots
                                to the centrepin of his body

He sets the little circlets on her fingertips
She stitches his body here and there
                                with steely purple silk
He oils the delicate cogs of her mouth
She inlays with deep-cuts scrolls the nape of his neck
He sinks into place the inside of her thighs

So, gasping with joy, with cries of wonderment
Like two gods of mud
Sprawling in the dirt, but with infinite care

They bring each other to perfection.

The Owl Flower

Big terror descends.

A drumming glare, a flickering face of flames.

Something writhes apart into a signal,
Fiendish, a filament of incandescence.

As it were a hair.

In the maelstrom's eye,
In the core of the brimming heaven-blossom,
Under the tightening whorl of plumes, a mote
Scalds in dews.

A leaf of the earth
Applies to it, a cooling health.

A coffin spins in the torque.
Wounds flush with sap, headful of pollen,
Wet with nectar
The dead one stirs.

A mummy grain is cracking its grimace
In the cauldron of tongues.

The ship of flowers
Nudges the wharf of skin.

The egg-stone
Bursts among broody petals —

And a staggering thing
Fired with rainbows, raw with cringing heat,

Blinks at the source.

The Risen

He stands, filling the doorway
In the shell of earth.

He lifts wings, he leaves the remains of something,
A mess of offal, muddled as an afterbirth.

His each wingbeat – a convict's release.
What he brings will be plenty.

He slips behind the world's brow
As music escapes its skull, its clock and its skyline.

Under his sudden shadow, flames cry out among thickets.
When he soars, his shape

Is a cross, eaten by light,
On the Creator's face.

He shifts world weirdly as sunspots
Emerge as earthquakes.

A burning unconsumed,
A whirling tree –

Where he alights
A skin sloughs from a leafless apocalypse.

On his lens
Each atom engraves with a diamond.

In the wind-fondled crucible of his splendour
The dirt becomes God.

But when will he land
On a man's wrist?

Finale

At the end of the ritual
                        up comes a goblin.

RIVER

For Nicholas

Salmon Eggs

The salmon were just down there –
Shivering together, touching at each other,
Shedding themselves for each other –

Now beneath flood-murmur
They peel away deathwards.

                    January haze,
With a veined yolk of sun. In bone-damp cold
I lean and watch the water, listening to water
Till my eyes forget me

And the piled flow supplants me, the mud-blooms

All this ponderous light of everlasting
Collapsing away under its own weight

Mastodon ephemera

Mud-curdling, bull-dozing, hem-twinkling
Caesarean of Heaven and Earth, unfelt

With exhumations and delirious advents –

                    Catkins
Wriggle at their mother's abundance. The spider clings to his
   craft.

Something else is going on in the river

More vital than death – death here seems a superficiality
Of small scaly limbs, parasitical. More grave than life
Whose reflex jaws and famished crystals
Seem incidental
To this telling – these tidings of plasm –
The melt of mouthing silence, the charge of light
Dumb with immensity.

           The river goes on
Sliding through its place, undergoing itself
In its wheel.

                I make out the sunk foundations
Of dislocated crypts, a bedrock
Time-hewn, time-riven altar. And this is the liturgy
Of Earth's coming – harrowing, crowned – a travail
Of raptures and rendings. Perpetual mass
Of the waters
Wells from the cleft.
             This is the swollen vent
Of the nameless
Teeming inside atoms – and inside the haze
And inside the sun and inside the earth.

It is the font, brimming with touch and whisper,
Swaddling the egg.
          Only birth matters
Say the river's whorls.
             And the river
Silences everything in a leaf-mouldering hush
Where sun rolls bare, and earth rolls,

And mind condenses on old haws.

Japanese River Tales

I

Tonight
From the swaddled village, down the padded lane
Snow is hurrying
To the tryst, is touching
At her hair, at her raiment
Glint-slippered
Over the stubble,
                  naked under
Her light robe, jewels
In her hair, in her ears, at her bare throat
Dark eye-flash
              twigs and brambles
Catch at her
          as she lifts
The raggy curtains
Of the river's hovel, and plunges
Into his grasping bed.

II

The lithe river rejoices all morning
In his juicy bride – the snow princess
Who peeped from clouds, and chose him,
                    and descended.

The tale goes on
With glittery laughter of immortals
Shaking the alders –
In the end a drowsy after-bliss
Blue-hazes the long valley. High gulls
Look down on the flash
And languor of suppled shoulders
Bedded in her ermine.
                    Night
Lifts off the illusion. Lifts
The beauty from her skull. The sockets, in fact,
Are root-arches – empty
To ashes of stars. Her kiss
Grips through the full throat and locks
On the dislodged vertebrae.
                    Her talons
Lengthened by moonlight, numb open
The long belly of blood.
                    And the river
Is a gutter of death,   .
A spill of glitters
                    dangling from her grasp
As she flies
Through the shatter of space and
Out of being.

Flesh of Light

From a core-flash, from a thunder-silence
In the sun – something has fallen.
It crawls in glair, among heather-topped stones.

Cattle stumble into it. Lift muzzles
Unspooling the glimmer.
Dark bodies dense with boiling light.

Something new-born crawls, a phosphorescence
Illuminates the underleaves of stolid
Oak and the quivering iris. Eyes of ova

Round and swell with the waters of hunger,
Hesitate and ease
Into focus, magnetized by light

In these coils of aura. You peer down
Into a self reflected, a spectre.
This is the sun's oiled snake, dangling, fallen,

The medicinal, mercury creature
Sheathed with the garb, in all its rainbow scales,
That it sheds

And refreshes, spasming and whispering.
Spinal cord of the prone, adoring land,
Rapt

To the roots of the sea,
To the blossoming
Of the sea.

The Merry Mink

                 — the Arctic Indian's
Black bagful of hunter's medicine —
Now has to shift for himself.

Since he's here, he's decided to like it.
Now it is my turn, he says,
To enjoy my pelt uselessly.

I am the Mighty Northern Night, he says,
In my folktale form.
See, I leave my stars at the river's brim.

Little Black Thundercloud, lost from his mythology,
A-boil with lightnings
He can't get rid of. He romps through the ramsons

(Each one like a constellation), topples into the river,
Jolly goblin, realist—optimist
(Even his trapped, drowned snake-head grins)

As if he were deathless. Bobs up
Ruffed with a tough primeval glee. Crams trout, nine together,
Into his bank-hole — his freezer —

Where they rot in three days. Makes love
Eight hours at a go.
                 My doings and my pelt,
He says, are a Platonic idea

Where I live with God.

Stump Pool in April

Crack willows in their first pale eclosion
Of emerald. The long pool
Is seething with oily lights. Deep labour
Embodied under filmy spanglings. Oxygen
Boils in its throat, and the new limbs
Flex and loosen. It keeps
Making the effort to burst its glistenings
With sinewy bulgings, gluey splittings
All down its living length.

              The river is trying
To rise out of the river.
             April
Has set its lights working. Its limp wings
Crease in their folds, hump and convulse
To lift out over the daffodils.
                 The soft strokings
Of south wind keep touching all its membranes
Into spasming torments. It knows
The time has come for it to alter
And to fly, and to fasten – in wedlock –
With the hill-wood waiting high there, flushed
In her bridal veil of haze-violet.

Whiteness

Walks the river at dawn.

The thorn-tree hiding its thorns
With too much and too fleshy perfume.

Thin water. Uneasy ghost.
Whorls clotted with petals.

Trout, like a hidden man's cough,
Slash under dripping roots.

Heron. Clang
Coiling its snake in heavy hurry
Hoists away, yanked away

Ceases to ponder the cuneiform
Under glass

Huge owl-lump of dawn
With wrong fittings, a parasol broken
Tumbles up into strong sky

Banks precariously, risks a look
A writhing unmade bedstead

Sets the blade between its shoulders
And hang-falls
Down a long aim

Dangles its reeds

Till it can see its own pale eyes

Suddenly shakes off cumbersome cloud
To anchor, tall,
An open question.

Now only the river nags to be elsewhere.

An August Salmon

Upstream and downstream, the river's closed.
Summer wastes in the pools.
A sunken calendar unfurls,
Fruit ripening as the petals rot.

A holed-up gangster,
He dozes, his head on the same stone,
Gazing towards the skylight,
Waiting for time to run out on him.

Alone, in a cellar of ash-roots,
The bridegroom, mortally wounded
By love and destiny,
Features deforming with deferment.

His beauty bleeding invisibly
From every lift of his gills.

He gulps, awkward in his ponderous regalia,
But his eye stays rapt,
Elephantine, Arctic –
A god, on earth for the first time,
With the clock of love and death in his body.

Four feet under weightless, premature leaf-crisps
Stuck in the sliding sky. Sometimes
A wind wags a bramble up there.

The pulsing tiny trout, so separately fated,
Glue themselves to the stones near him.

His tail-frond, the life-root,
Fondling the poor flow, stays him
On the torpedo launch of his poise –
Sleeked ice, a smear of being
Over his anchor shadow.

       Monkish, caressed
He kneels. He bows
Into the ceaseless gift
That unwinds the spool of his strength.

Dusk narrows too quickly. Manic-depressive
Unspent, poltergeist anti-gravity
Spins him in his pit, levitates him
Through a fountain of plate glass,

Reveals his dragonized head,
The March-flank's ice-floe soul-flash
Rotted to a muddy net of bruise,
Flings his coil at the remainder of light –

Red-black and nearly unrecognizable,
He drops back, helpless with weight,
Tries to shake loose the riveted skull
And its ghoul decor –

                sinks to the bed
Of his wedding cell, the coma waiting
For execution and death
In the skirts of his bride.

Fairy Flood

A brown musically moving beauty, the earth's fullness
Slides towards the sea. An escape
Of earth-serpent, with all its hoards, casting the land, like an
    old skin,
Pulling its body from under the eye.

                                        Escaping daughter
Her whole glass castle melting about her
In full magic –

Some mask of crumpling woe disfigures
Her deep liberation, which is actually jubilant,
As she brings down earth and sky blamelessly
In this headlong elopement without finery,
Weeps past – a freed out-heaping
Of accusative love and abandon.

The fatherly landscape upbraids and harangues,
Claws weakly at her swollen decision
With gaping beard and disarrayed robe,
Undoes his stained bandages,
Exposes his bone-open wounds –

The river cries out once, tosses her hair, hides her eyes,
Bleeding him empty remorselessly.

The West Dart

It spills from the Milky Way, spiked with light,
It fuses the flash-gripped earth —

The spicy torrent, that seems to be water
Which is spirit and blood.

A violet glance of lightning
Melts the granite to live glass,
Pours it into the mould of quick moor-water

A trout swipes its flank at the thundercloud

A shatter of crowns, a tumbling out of goblets

Where the slag of world crumbles cooling
In thunders and rainy portents.

1984 on 'The Tarka Trail'

I

The river is suddenly green – dense bottle green.
Hard in the sun, dark as spinach.
Drought pools bleach their craters.
The river's floor is a fleece –
Tresses of some vile stuff
That disintegrates to a slime as you touch it
Leaving your fingers fouled with a stink of diesel.

The river's glutted – a boom of plenty for algae.
A festering olla podrida, poured slowly.
Surfactants, ammonia, phosphates – the whole banquet
Flushed in by sporadic thunderbursts
But never a flood enough to scour a sewer,
Never enough to resurrect a river.

A bottleful is like sap, a rich urine,
With minuscule flying saucers whizzing in it.
Down near the estuary – this goes into the mains.
But nothing can help the patient. In the August afternoon
The golden picnic sunrays, leaning dustily
Through the conifers, gaze down
At a ditch-carcase, a puddled horror –
Bile draining from rags, the hulk of ribs.

Charlie found a stranded mussel. He brought it
Up the fishing ladder.
The lips gaped. We peered in, and pried wider,
Parted her pearly gates to get a peek
At her curtained uvula: Queen of the River
Still in her silken chamber, or was it – ?
A yawn of putrid phlegm.

Then the stench hit us. He yelled
And flailed it from his fingers as if it had burnt him
Into a blaze of willow-herb
'God! The river's dead! Oh God!
Even the mussels are finished!'

The tale of a dying river
Does not end where you stand with the visitors
At a sickbed, feeling the usual
Nothing more than mangled helplessness.
You cannot leave this hospital because
Peter, the good corn farmer, with his three plus
Tons of quality grain to the acre (behind him
The Min. of Ag. and Fish.'s hard guarantee
Which is the hired assurance of hired science)
Heaps the poisons into you too.

His upriver neighbour – just as overwhelmed –
Wades through slurry and silage. Where his dad
Milked a herd of twenty, he milks ninety –
Oozing effluent 'equal to the untreated
Sewage of a city the size of Gloucester'.

But Peter, our clean corn farmer, nature protector,
Striding between lush hedgebanks he lets go bush
To gladden the spider, past his carefully nursed
Neglected nettles (a crèche for the butterflies),
The birdwatcher, binoculars thumping his sternum,
Has measured his medicines towards that maximum yield
Into your dish for years. Yes, and smiled
Up towards the colluding sun. And returned
Over his corn (which now, near ripe, seems burned
Oak-dark with some fungus) thirteen times
Between the drill and the reaper.

Three hundredweight of 20–10–10 to the acre,
A hundredweight and a half straight Nitram.
Pesticides, herbicides, fungicides, the grand slam –
Each time twenty gallons to the acre
Into your dish, with top-ups. And slug-pellets
A bonus, with the rest, into your cup
(Via the lifeless ditch – meaning your tap).
Now you are as loaded with the data
That cultivate his hopes, in this brief gamble
As this river is –
            as he is too,
He can't escape either, nor can his lively young wife,
Who laughs if you ask them why they do what they do
(Her voice ventriloqual, her shoulders jerking on their strings)
'But the children have to be educated.'

II

   Nymet

No map or Latin ever
Netted one deity from this river.
Taw meant simply *water*.
What was her true name

When with yellow smoky nettle pollen
And the first thorn's confetti
She crushed the May bridegroom's
Head into her flood?

Afterwards she bore him, unfailing,
All summer the splendour
Of eel-wreaths, the glut of white peal,
The glow-cold, sea-new salmon.

Deepening together
Her coombe and her name.
Where is she now?
A fairy

Drowned in the radioactive Irish Sea.
Blood-donor
To the South West Water Authority.
Her womb's been requisitioned

For the cloacal flux, the accountancy curse
Of the Express Dairy Cheese Factory –
'Biggest In Europe'.
A miasma

Mourns on the town bridge, at odd hours,
Over her old home, now her grave.
That's her.
She rots

But still stirs – a nightly, dewy spectre,
Nameless revenant
In her grave-shroud, resurrected
By her maternal despair

For her doomed parr. She wipes their lips
Of the stuff that weeps
From her curdled dug since it became
The fistula of a thousand farms. That's her –

Now she truly can be called: Sewer.
(More truly: The Washer at the Ford.
As in the old story.
The death-rags that she washes and washes are ours.)

Ophelia

Where the pool unfurls its undercloud —
There she goes.

And through and through
The kneading tumble and the water-hammer.

If a trout leaps into air, it is not for a breather.
It has to drop back immediately

Into this peculiar engine
That made it, and keeps it going,

And that works it to death —
                              there she goes

Darkfish, finger to her lips,
Staringly into the afterworld.

Be a Dry-Fly Purist

Barely prick the meniscus. Lightly caress
The last gleam on the river. Lift off deftly
As a sedge-fly. Keep your head clear
Keep your body keep your soul clear

Of the river-fetch —
                    (the epileptic's strobe,
The yell of the Muezzin
Or the 'Bismillah!'
That spins the dancer in

Her whole body liquefied
Where a body loves to be
Rapt in the river of its own music) —

Or be lost.
            (*And she said:*
                        '*When I hooked*
My first salmon, that salmon
In the Ferry Pool, it was I never
Expected nobody ever told I had never
Known anything not
Riding over jumps all I could think it
Was like having my first baby — ')

A Rival

The cormorant, commissar of the hard sea,
Has not adjusted to the soft river.

He lifts his pterodactyl head in the drought pool
(Sound-proof cellar of final solutions).

The dinosaur massacre-machine
Hums on in his skull, programme unaltered.

That fossil eye-chip could reduce
All the blood in the world, yet still taste nothing.

At dawn he's at it, under the sick face –
Cancer in the lymph, uncontrollable.

Level your eye's aim and he's off
Knocking things over, out through the window –

An abortion-doctor
Black bag packed with vital organs

Dripping unspeakably.
                            Then away, heavy, high
Over the sea's iron curtain –

The pool lies there mutilated,
                            face averted,
Dumb and ruined.

Dee

The hills locked in snow
Have locked up their springs. The shining paps
That nurse the river's plumpness
Are locked up.
And the North Star is frozen in its lock.

The expenditure of swift purity
Nevertheless goes on. But so thinly,
So meanly, and from such stale cellars
No fish will face it.
Somewhere the salmon have turned back into the sea.

So this is the majesty of the April Dee
When the snowdrops, pert and apart,
Domes of ice-light, deviants
From a world preoccupied with water,
Hurt into perfection, steal a summer
Out of the old, river-worried
Carcase of winter.

Nothing else dare or can
Pilfer from the shrunk, steely procession.

Nevertheless, the lit queenliness of snow hills,
The high, frozen bosom, wears this river
Like a peculiarly fine jewel.

Salmon-Taking Times

After a routing flood-storm, the river
Was a sounder of loud muddy pigs
Flushed out of hillsides. Tumbling hooligans
They jammed the old bends. Diabolical muscle,
Piglets, tusky boars, possessed, huge sows
Piling in the narrows.

                I stayed clear. 'Swine
Bees and women cannot be turned.'

                But after
The warm shower
That just hazed and softened the daffodil buds
And clotted the primroses, a gauze
Struggles tenderly in the delighted current –
Clambers wetly on stones, and the river emerges
In glistenings, and gossamer, bridal veils,
And hovers over itself – there is a wedding
Delicacy –
              so delicate
I touch it and its beauty-frailty crumples
To a smear of wet, a strengthless wreckage
Of dissolving membranes – and the air is ringing.

It is like a religious moment, slightly dazing.

It is like a shower of petals of eglantine.

Earth-Numb

Dawn – a smouldering fume of dry frost,
Sky-edge of red-hot iron.
Daffodils motionless – some fizzled out.
The birds – earth-brim simmering.
Sycamore buds unsticking – the leaf out-crumpling, purplish.

The pheasant's cock's glare cry. Jupiter ruffling softly.

Hunting salmon. And hunted
And haunted by apparitions from tombs
Under the smoothing tons of dead element
In the river's black canyons.

The lure is a prayer. And my searching
Like the slow sun.
A prayer, like a flower opening.
A surgeon operating
On an open heart, with needles –

And bang! the river grabs at me

A mouth-flash, an electrocuting malice
Like a trap, trying to rip life off me –
And the river stiffens alive,
The black pit thumps, the whole river hauls,

A piling voltage hums, jamming me stiff –

Something terrified and terrifying
Gleam-surges to and fro through me
From the river to the sky, from the sky into the river

Uprooting dark bedrock, shatters it in air
Cartwheels across me, slices thudding through me
As if I were the current –

Till the fright flows all one way down the line

And a ghost grows solid, a hoverer,
A lizard-green slither, banner heavy.

Then the wagging stone pebble-head
Trying to think on shallows.

Then the steel spectre of purples
From the forge of water
Gagging on emptiness

As the eyes of incredulity
Fix their death-exposure of the celandine and the cloud.

Caddis

Struggle-drudge – with the ideas of a crocodile
And the physique of a foetus.

Absurd mudlark – living your hovel's life –
Yourself your own worst obstacle.

Lugging Castle Paranoia
Through that moonland, like a train off its track,

Under the river's hurricane.
You should have been a crab. It's no good.

Trout in March are crammed
With the debris of your hopeful redoubts.

Wasp-face, orphaned and a waif too early,
Improvising – with inaudible war-cries –

This Herculean makeshift, hoisting your house,
You can nip my finger but

You are still a baby.
Your alfresco Samurai suit of straws,

Your Nibelungen mail of agates, affirms
Only fantasies of fear and famine.

Hurry up. Join the love-orgy
Up here among leaves, in the light rain,

Under a flimsy tent of dusky wings.

The Gulkana

The Gulkana, where it meets the Copper,
Swung, jade, out of the black spruce forest,
And disappeared into it.

Away to the north, jumbled iceberg hills
And a long wreath of fire-haze.

Fine word, Gulkana. What does it mean?
A pre-Columbian glyph.
A pale blue thread – scrawled with a child's hand
Across our map.
                    We stumbled, not properly awake,
In a weird light – a bombardment
Of ultra-violet,
Among phrases that lumped out backwards. Among rocks
That kept startling me – too rock-like,
Hypnagogic rocks –
                    A scrapyard of boxy shacks
And supermarket refuse, dogs, wrecked pick-ups
The Indian village where we bought our pass
Was comatose – on the stagnation toxins
Of a cultural vasectomy. They were relapsing
To Cloud-like-a-Boulder, Mica, Bear, Magpie.

We hobbled along a tightrope shore of pebbles
Under a trickling bluff
That bounced the odd pebble on to us, eerily.
(The whole land in perpetual seismic tremor.)
And this was the Gulkana –
Biblical, a deranging cry
From the wilderness, burst past us
And dragged at us. I found myself clinging

To the lifted skyline fringe of rag spruce
And the subsidence under my bootsoles
With balancing glances. Almost a fear
Something I kept trying to deny

Made my steps strange to me. It stayed with me
As if it rode on my pack –
A nape-of-the-neck unease. I'd sploshed far enough
Through the spongy sinks of the permafrost
For this river's
Miraculous fossils – creatures that each midsummer
Resurrected through it, in a blood-rich flesh.
Pilgrims for a fish!
Prospectors for the lode in a fish's eye!

In the strange violet light, that mercury light,
My illusion developed. I felt hunted.
I tested the fear. It seemed to live in my neck –
A craven, bird-headed alertness.
And in my eye
That felt blind somehow to what I stared at
As if it stared at me. And in my ear –
So wary of the air-stir in the spruce-tips
My ear-drum almost ached. I explained it
To my quietly arguing, lucid panic
As my fear of one inside me,
A bodiless twin, some doppelgänger
Disinherited other, unliving,
Ever-living, a larva from prehistory,
Whose journey this was, who now exulted
Recognizing his home,
And whose gaze I could feel as he watched me

Fiddling with my gear – the interloper,
The fool he had always hated. We pitched our tent

And for three days
Our tackle scratched the windows of the express torrent.

We seemed underpowered. Whatever we hooked
Bent in air, a small porpoise,
Then went straight downriver under the weight
And joined the glacial landslide of the Copper
Which was the colour of cement.

Even when we got one ashore
It was too big to eat.

But there was the eye!
                    I peered into that lens
Seeking what I had come for. (What had I come for?
The camera-flash? The burned-out, ogling bulb?)
What I saw was small, crazed, snake-like.
It made me think of a dwarf, shrunken sun
And of the black, refrigerating pressures
Under the Bering Sea.

We relaunched their mulberry-dark torsos,
Those gulping, sooted mouths, the glassy visors –

Arks of an undelivered covenant,
Egg-sacs of their own Eden,

Seraphs of heavy ore
They surged away, magnetized,
Into the furnace boom of the Gulkana.

Bliss had fixed their eyes
Like an anaesthetic. They were possessed
By that voice in the river

And its accompaniment —
The flutes, the drumming. And they rose and sank
Like voices, like singers themselves
In its volume. We watched them, deepening away.
They looked like what they were — somnambulists,
Drugged, ritual victims — melting from us
Towards a sacrament
                    a consummation
That could only be death.
Which it would be, within some numbered days.
In a spillway, where a man could hardly stand,
These aboriginal Americans,
High among rains, in an opening of the hills,
Will begin to circle
In shufflings and shudders, male by female,
Begin to dance their deaths —
The current hosing over their brows and shoulders,
Bellies riven open and shaken empty
Into the gutter of pebbles
In an orgy of eggs and sperm,
The dance orgy of being reborn
From which masks and regalia drift empty,
Torn off — at last their very bodies,
In the numbed, languorous frenzy, as obstacles,
Ripped away —
                    ecstasy dissolving
In the mercy of water, at the star of the source,
Devoured by revelation,
Every molecule seized, and tasted and drained
Into that amethyst of emptiness —

I came back to myself. A spectre
Lifted my quivering coffee, in the aircraft,
And sipped at it. Adrift, convalescent,
I imagined our aircraft
As if a small boy held it
Making its noise. And a spectre,
Escaping the film's flicker, peered from the porthole
Under the sun's cobalt darkness
Down on to Greenland's corpse
Tight-sheeted with snow-glare.

                          Word by word
The voice of the river moved in me.
It was like lovesickness. Like a mourning
Numbness, a secret bleeding, a deeper
Waking in my body.

                         Telling of the King
Salmon's eye.

                 Of the blood-mote mosquito.

And the stilt-legged, subarctic, one-rose rose
With its mock aperture, tilting toward us
In our tent doorway, its needle tremor.

And the old Indian Headman, in his tatty jeans and socks, who
    smiled
Adjusting to our incomprehension – his face
A whole bat, that glistened and stirred.

Madly Singing in the Mountains

For John Montague

The water-skeeter is old. As the sunlight
That microscopes the quartzes
In his quarried, water-walking body
Is old.

The whole crooked river is old. And the land
It lies down with is as old. The rocks
That it quarrels with, that quarrel with it,
That it embraces, that embrace it
Are as old.

                    This marriage is old.

Old are the elvers. Old are all ephemerids
That will float away sealed flat as fossils
In the water-skin tomorrow.

The river and her family are so old
They have lost their way in our age.
Time has given up trying to find them.

Here in their first childhood, wrinkled ancients,
They sun themselves
Or roam in the weather
Still singing the songs time can't touch.

Go Fishing

Join water, wade in underbeing
Let brain mist into moist earth
Ghost loosen away downstream
Gulp river and gravity

Lose words
Cease
Be assumed into glistenings of lymph
As if creation were a wound
As if this flow were all plasm healing

Be supplanted by mud and leaves and pebbles
By sudden rainbow monster-structures
That materialize in suspension gulping
And dematerialize under pressure of the eye

Be cleft by the sliding prow
Displaced by the hull of light and shadow

Dissolved in earth-wave, the soft sun-shock,
Dismembered in sun-melt

Become translucent – one untangling drift
Of water-mesh, and a weight of earth-taste light
Mangled by wing-shadows
Everything circling and flowing and hover-still

Crawl out over roots, new and nameless
Search for face, harden into limbs

Let the world come back, like a white hospital
Busy with urgency words

Try to speak and nearly succeed
Heal into time and other people

If

If the sky is infected
The river has to drink it

If earth has a disease which could be fatal
The river has to drink it

If you have infected the sky and the earth
Caught its disease off you – you are the virus

If the sea drinks the river
And the earth drinks the sea

It is one quenching and one termination

If your blood is trying to clean itself
In the filter of your corrupted flesh
And the sores run – that is the rivers

The five rivers of Paradise

Where will you get a pure drink now?

Already – the drop has returned to the cup

Already you are your ditch, and there you drink

The Bear

For Alan Hancox

The day darkened in rain. In the bottom of the gorge
The big tarp awning we sat approximately under
Bucked in its ropes. Pans took off.
Nothing we could do
Could alter anything. River rising by the minute.
The rapids churning fog. Ron came in:
'The rain's warm! Feel the warmth of that wind!'

The mountains stood above us in their saunas.
Our flood-indicators were the cataracts
Dangling down their chests and faces
From under their hoods of snow.

When would the rain end?
Maybe it wouldn't, maybe this was The Rains –
The winter coming early. Maybe the river
Never would surrender Ehor's wine-cache
Already four feet under the sliding concrete
Till maybe next June. So why were we happy?
How could we get out? We couldn't.
What else could we be doing? Nothing.
Hands tight hidden, hats down over our ears.
Patience welled up like a comfort.
And Life, said Jay, is simple – just a clock
Of good cooking and even better coffee.
And of calculating, shouted Ehor,
By those heavenly egg-timers above us
Occasionally to be glimpsed through the cloud-rags,
And by the deepening bow-wave of that log-jam
What a fantastic upriver flood of Steelhead

This will leave us to deal with!
This gloomy wash-out, my friends, is our bonanza!
And the streamy danglers
That decorate the mountains' Indian faces
Mean the rain is getting excited for us
And wanting the mountains to dance. It has dressed the
    mountains
For a dance – the dance of the Steelhead,
The rain-storm dance, the snow-melt. Those ribbons
Are our dance regalia –

We could have appreciated it all,
We could have let the spirits, clamped in our weatherproofs,
Magnify themselves and dance with the mountains
And the whirling wind in robes
Of rain and elemental nostalgia –
But what those busy tickertapes were telling
Was bigger water, river out of control,
The Steelhead hugging deeper
As if they were under an avalanche
Their more and more unthinkable finger-holds,
While our fishing days and our flown-in dreams
Rumbled away over them tossing driftwood,
Bleeding us downstream. Our dance was to sit tight,
Freshly sawn-off stumps, hugging our roots,
Stumps of abandoned sawn-off totem poles
At a glum remove from our enterprise
Suspended in the clouds literally,
Clouds that were dragging up and down the gorge
Simultaneously in opposite directions,
A dance that mimed the hope of hopelessness
To squalls that slapped gunshots out of the tent,
Our gossip out of our mouths, and scattered our coffee.

While rain ripped at the tarp. And taps were spluttering
At every corner – every edge tasselled or bucketing
As the tarp jumped. And dangledrops were descending
Along every cord, or snapped off.
We could only watch it all and know
Everything was worsening.

                    But we sat there
And enjoyed it. And the Steelhead down there
They were enjoying it too, this was what they were made of,
And made by, and made for, this was their moment.
The thousand-mile humping of mountains
That looked immovable, was in a frenzy,
Metabolism of stars, melt of snows –
Was shivering to its ecstasy in the Steelhead.
This actually was the love-act that had brought them
Out of everywhere, squirming and leaping,
And that had brought us too – besotted voyeurs –
Trying to hook ourselves into it.
And all the giddy orgasm of the river
Quaking under our feet –

                    'What's that? It's a bear!'
A black snag reeled past on the blue-white swirls – a tree root?
'It's a goddamned bear!' It was a bear.
The night before's mystery upstream gunshot
Materialized, saluted us, and vanished
As a black sea-going bear, a scapegoat, an offering.

The River

Fallen from heaven, lies across
The lap of his mother, broken by world.

But water will go on
Issuing from heaven

In dumbness uttering spirit brightness
Through its broken mouth.

Scattered in a million pieces and buried
Its dry tombs will split, at a sign in the sky,

At a rending of veils.
It will rise, in a time after times,

After swallowing death and the pit
It will return stainless

For the delivery of this world.
So the river is a god

Knee-deep among reeds, watching men,
Or hung by the heels down the door of a dam

It is a god, and inviolable.
Immortal. And will wash itself of all deaths.

Under the Hill of Centurions

The river is in a resurrection fever.
Now at Easter you find them
Up in the pool's throat, and in the very jugular
Where the stickle pulses under grasses –

Cock minnows!

They have abandoned contemplation and prayer in the pool's
    crypt.

There they are, packed all together,
In an inch of seething light.

A stag-party, all bridegrooms, all in their panoply –

Red-breasted as if they bled, their Roman
Bottle-glass greened bodies silked with black

In the clatter of the light loom of water
All singing and
Toiling together,
Wreathing their metals
Into the warp and weft of the lit water –

I imagine their song,
Deep-chested, striving, solemn.

A wrestling tress of kingfisher colour,
Steely jostlings, a washed mass of brilliants

Labouring at earth
In the wheel of light –

Ghostly rinsings
A struggle of spirits.

Stealing Trout on a May Morning

I park the car half in the ditch and switch off and sit.
The hot astonishment of my engine's arrival
Sinks through 5 a.m. silence and frost.
At the end of a long gash
An atrocity through the lace of first light
I sit with the reeking instrument.
I am on delicate business.
I want the steel to be cold instantly
And myself secreted three fields away
And the farms, back under their blankets, supposing a plane
   passed.

Because this is no wilderness you can just rip into.
Every leaf is plump and well-married,
Every grain of soil of known lineage, well-connected.
And the gardens are like brides fallen asleep
Before their weddings have properly begun.
The orchards are the hushed maids, fresh from convent –
It is too hushed, something improper is going to happen.
It is too ghostly proper, all sorts of liveried listenings
Tiptoe along the lanes and peer over hedges.

I listen for the eyes jerked open on pillows,
Their dreams washed with sudden ugly petroleum.
They need only look out at a sheep.
Every sheep within two miles
Is nailing me accurately down
With its hellishly shaven starved-priest expression.

I emerge. The air, after all, has forgotten everything.
The sugared spindles and wings of grass
Are etched on great goblets. A pigeon falls into space.

The earth is coming quietly and darkly up from a great depth,
Still under the surface. I am unknown,
But nothing is surprised. The tarmac of the road
Is velvet with sleep, the hills are out cold.
A new earth still in its wrappers
Of gauze and cellophane,
The frost from the storage still on its edges,
My privilege to poke and sniff.
The sheep are not much more than the primroses.
And the river there, amazed with itself,
Flexing and trying its lights
And unused fish, that are rising
And sinking for the sheer novelty
As the sun melts the hill's spine and the spilled light
Flows through their gills . . .

My mind sinks, rising and sinking.
And the opening arms of the sky forget me
Into the buried tunnels of hazels. There
My boot dangles down, till a thing black and sudden
Savages it, and the river is heaping under,
Alive and malevolent,
A coiling glider of shock, the space-black
Draining off the night-moor, under the hazels –
But I drop and stand square in it, against it,
Then it is river again, washing its soul,
Its stones, its weeds, its fish, its gravels
And the rooty mouths of the hazels clear
Of the discolourings bled in
Off ploughlands and lanes . . .

At first, I can hardly look at it –
The riding tables, the corrugated
Shanty roofs tightening

To braids, boilings where boulders throw up
Gestures of explosion, black splitting everywhere
To drowning skirts of whiteness, a slither of mirrors
Under the wading hazels. Here it is shallow,
Ropes my knees, lobbing fake boomerangs,
A drowned woman loving each ankle,
But I'm heavier and I wade with them upstream,
Flashing my green minnow
Up the open throats of water
And across through the side of the rush
Of alligator escaping along there
Under the beards of the hazels, and I slice
The wild nape-hair off the bald bulges,
Till the tightrope of my first footholds
Tangles away downstream
And my bootsoles move as to magnets.

Soon I deepen. And now I meet the piling mob
Of voices and hurriers coming towards me
And tumbling past me. I press through a panic –
This headlong river is a rout
Of tumbrils and gun-carriages, rags and metal,
All the funeral woe-drag of some overnight disaster
Mixed with planets, electrical storms and darkness
On a mapless moorland of granite,
Trailing past me with all its frights, its eyes
With what they have seen and still see,
They drag the flag off my head, a dark insistence
Tearing the spirits from my mind's edge and from under . . .

To yank me clear takes the sudden, strong spine
Of one of the river's real members –
Thoroughly made of dew, lightning and granite
Very slowly over four years. A trout, a foot long,

Lifting its head in a shawl of water,
Fins banked stiff like a schooner
It forces the final curve wide, getting
A long look at me. So much for the horror:
It has changed places.
        Now I am a man in a painting
(Under the mangy, stuffed head of a fox)
Painted about 1905
Where the river steams and the frost relaxes
On the pear-blossoms. The brassy wood-pigeons
Bubble their colourful voices, and the sun
Rises upon a world well-tried and old.

The Moorhen

Might not notice you.
She's policing the water-bugs
In her municipal uniform.

A watchful clockwork
Jerks her head ahead, to inspect ahead
At each deep tread
Of her giant ooze-treading clawspread.

Her undertail flirts, jerk by jerk,
A chevron blaze, her functionary flash,
And the blood-orange badge or bleb
On her helmet neb
Lets the transgressing water-skeeter know
The arresting face, the stabbing body-blow
Is official.

Her legs are still primeval –
Toy-grotesque
As when she – thistledown, black, tip-toe –
Scampered across the picture-skin of water.

Lumpier now, she sprint-strides into flight
Across stepping-stones of slapped circles

Then dangles her drape of webs below her
Like a hawthorn fly, till she hoicks up
Clear over the bulrush plumes, and crash-drops

Into her off-duty nervous collapse.

September Salmon

Famously home from sea,
Nobly preoccupied with his marriage licence,
He ignores the weir's wrangle. Ignores
The parochial down-drag
Of the pool's long diphthong. Ignores
Festivals of insect fluorescence.

He serves his descendants. And his homage
Is to be patient, performing, slowly, the palsy
Of concerted autumn
In the upside-down cage of a tree.

Does he envy the perennial eels and the mongrel minnows?
He is becoming a god,
A tree of sexual death, sacred with lichens.

Sometimes, for days, lost to himself.
                              Mid-morning,
At the right angle of sun
You can see the floor of his chapel.
There he sways at the altar –
A soul
Hovering in the incantation and the incense.

Over his sky the skeeters traffic, godlike and double-jointed.
He lifts
To the molten palate of the mercurial light
And adds his daub.

The Mayfly is Frail

The way the shivering Northern Lights are frail.

Erupting floods, flood-lava drag across farms,
Oak-roots cartwheeling –
The inspiration was seismic.

Some mad sculptor
In frenzy remaking the river's rooms
Through days and nights of bulging shoulders
And dull bellowing – cooled with cloudbursts –
Needed all his temperament.

Now he sprawls – flat in the sun –
Apparently burned out.

And now comes the still small voice.

Out of his glowing exhaustion
Heals a giddy mote,
A purity in a mould

And the mould splits at a touch of the air.

A shimmering beast
Dawns from the river's opened side.

A Cormorant

Here before me, snake-head
My waders weigh seven pounds.

My Barbour jacket, mainly necessary
For its pockets, is proof

Against the sky at my back. My bag
Sags with lures and hunter's medicine enough

For a year in the Pleistocene.
My hat, of use only

If this May relapses to March,
Embarrasses me, and my net, long as myself,

Optimistic, awkward, infatuated
With every twig-snag and fence-barb

Will slowly ruin the day. I paddle
Precariously on slimed shale,

And infiltrate twenty yards
Of gluey and magnetized spider-gleam

Into the elbowing dense jostle-traffic
Of the river's tunnel, and pray

With futuristic, archaic under-breath
So that some fish, telepathically overpowered,

Will attach its incomprehension
To the bauble I offer to space in general.

The cormorant eyes me, beak uptilted,
Body snake-low — sea-serpentish.

He's thinking: 'Will that stump
Stay a stump just while I dive?' He dives.

He sheds everything from his tail end
Except fish-action, becomes fish,

Disappears from bird,
Dissolving himself

Into fish, so dissolving fish naturally
Into himself. Re-emerges, gorged,

Himself as he was, and escapes me.
Leaves me high and dry in my space-armour,

A deep-sea diver in two inches of water.

River Barrow

The light cools. Sun going down clear
Red-molten glass-blob, into green ember crumble
Of hill trees, over the Barrow
Where the flushed ash-grey sky lies perfect.

A skull tower is a nameless tomb. We sprawl
Rods out, giant grasshopper antennae, listening
For the bream-shoal to engage us.
                                        The current
Hauls its foam-line feed-lane
Along under the far bank – a furrow
Driving through heavy wealth,
Dragging a syrupy strength, a down-roping
Of the living honey.
                              It's an ancient thirst
Savouring all this, at the day's end,
Soaking it all up, through every membrane,
As if the whole body were a craving mouth,
As if a hunted ghost were drinking – sud-flecks
Grass-bits and omens
Fixed in the glass.
                              Trees inverted
Even in this sliding place are perfect.
All evil suspended. Flies
Teem over my hands, twanging their codes
In and out of my ear's beam. Future, past,
Reading each other in the water mirror
Barely tremble the thick nerve.
                                        Heavy belly
Of river, solid mystery
With a living vein. Odd trout

Flash-plop, curdle the molten,
Rive a wound in the smooth healing.
Over the now pink-lit ballroom glass
Tiny sedge-flies partner their shadows.

A wobbly, wavering balance of light
Mercury precarious in its sac
Leans to the weir's edge, spilling. Dog-bark stillness.
A wood-pigeon is buffing the far edges
Of the smoothing peace.
                              Great weight
Resting effortless on the weightless.
A cow's moo moves through the complex
Of internestled metals, a moon-spasm
Through interfolded underseas. I lie here,
Half-unearthed, an old sword in its scabbard,
Happy to moulder. Only the river moves.

Feet prickling in my tight-sock gumboots,
Hair itching with midges, blood easy
As this river. Honeysuckle
Pouring its horns of plenty over us
From the thickets behind.
                              A big fish,
Bream-roll or evening salmon, crashes
A crater of suds, and the river widens.

A long-armed spider readjusts his gunsights
Between glumes of over-leaning river-grass.

Midge bites itching and swelling.

Catadrome

Where does the river come from?
And the eel, the night-mind of water –
The river within the river and opposite –
The night-nerve of water?

Not from the earth's remembering mire
Not from the air's whim
Not from the brimming sun. Where from?

From the bottom of the nothing pool
Sargasso of God
Out of the empty spiral of stars

A glimmering person

Milesian Encounter on the Sligachan

For Hilary and Simon

'Up in the pools,' they'd said, and 'Two miles upstream.'

Something sinister about bogland rivers.

And a shock –

      after the two miles of tumblequag, of Ice-Age
      hairiness, crusty, quaking cadaver and me lurching
      over it in elation like a daddy-long-legs –

      after crooked little clatterbrook and again
      clatterbrook (a hurry of shallow grey light so
      distilled it looked like acid) –

      and after the wobbly levels of a razor-edged,
      blood-smeared grass, the flood-sucked swabs of bog-
        cotton,
      the dusty calico rip-up of snipe –

      under those petrified scapulae, vertebrae, horn-skulls
      the Cuillins (asylum of eagles) that were blue-silvered
      like wrinkled baking foil in the blue noon that day, and
      tremulous –

      early August, in a hot lateness (only three hours
      before my boat), a glimpse of my watch and suddenly

      up to my hip in a suck-hole then on again teetering over
      the broken-necked heath-bobs a good half-hour and me
      melting in my combined fuel of toil and
        clobber suddenly

The shock.
The sheer cavern of current piling silence
Under my feet.

So lonely-drowning deep, so drowned-hair silent
So clear
Cleansing the body cavity of the underbog.

Such a brilliant cut-glass interior
Sliding under me

And I felt a little bit giddy
Ghostly
As I fished the long pool-tail
Peering into that superabundance of spirit.

And now where were they, my fellow aliens from prehistory?
Those peculiar eyes
So like mine, but fixed at zero,
Pressing in from outer darkness
Eyes of aimed sperm and of egg on their errand,
Looking for immortality
In the lap of a broken volcano, in the furrow of a lost glacier,
Those shuttles of love-shadow?

Only humbler beings waved at me –
Weeds grazing the bottom, idling their tails.

Till the last pool –
A broad, coiling whorl, a deep ear
Of pondering amber,
Greenish and precious like a preservative,
With a ram's skull sunk there – magnified, a Medusa,
Funereal, phosphorescent, a lamp
Ten feet under the whisky.

I heard this pool whisper a warning.

I tickled its leading edges with temptation.
I stroked its throat with a whisker.
I licked the moulded hollows
Of its collarbones
Where the depth, now underbank opposite,
Pulsed up from contained excitements —

Eerie how you know when it's coming —
So I felt it now, my blood
Prickling and thickening, altering
With an ushering-in of chills, a weird onset
As if mountains were pushing mountains higher
Behind me, to crowd over my shoulder —

Then the pool lifted a travelling bulge
And grabbed the tip of my heart-nerve, and crashed,

Trying to wrench it from me, and again
Lifted a flash of arm for leverage
And it was a Gruagach of the Sligachan!
Some Boggart up from a crack in the granite!
A Glaistig out of the skull!
                              — what was it gave me
Such a supernatural, beautiful fright

And let go, and sank disembodied
Into the eye-pupil darkness?

Only a little salmon.
                    Salmo salar
The loveliest, left-behind, most-longed-for ogress

Of the Palaeolithic
Watched me through her time-warped judas-hole
In the ruinous castle of Skye

As I faded from the light of reality.

High Water

In the cragged pool
The river-smithy
Goes on labouring all night.

River-goblins
Toil the bellows, in the underglow.

Sledge-hammers of big water, rock anvils
Pound in the den of glooms.

With fling of glare metals and shadow-struggle.

Under the corrugated roof
Bulging and flashing mares
Slam down their heels, and are held.

Electrical stallions
Surge and, with oaths, are quieted.

A string of the sea's Arctic horses
Came up yesterday, with the salmon,
To be doctored, to be groomed, to be shod.

Two days, and the pool will be idle again.

Low Water

This evening
The river is a beautiful idle woman.

The day's August burn-out has distilled
A heady sundowner.
She lies back, bored and tipsy.

She lolls on her deep couch. And a long thigh
Lifts from the flash of her silks.

Adoring trees, kneeling, ogreish eunuchs
Comb out her spread hair, massage her fingers.

She stretches – and an ecstasy tightens
Over her skin, and deep in her gold body

Thrills spasm and dissolve. She drowses.

Her half-dreams lift out of her, light-minded
Love-pact suicides. Copulation and death.

She stirs her love-potion – ooze of balsam
Thickened with fish-mucus and algae.

You stand under leaves, your feet in shallows.
She eyes you steadily from the beginning of the world.

Night Arrival of Sea-Trout

Honeysuckle hanging her fangs.
Foxglove rearing her open belly.
Dogrose touching the membrane.

Through the dew's mist, the oak's mass
Comes plunging, tossing dark antlers.

Then a shattering
Of the river's hole, where something leaps out –

An upside-down, buried heaven
Snarls, moon-mouthed, and shivers.

Summer dripping stars, biting at the nape.
Lobworms coupling in saliva.
Earth singing under her breath.

And out in the hard corn a horned god
Running and leaping
With a bat in his drum.

An Eel

The strange part is his head. Her head. The strangely ripened
Domes over the brain, swollen nacelles
For some large containment. Lobed glands
Of some large awareness. Eerie the eel's head.
This full, plum-sleeked fruit of evolution.
Beneath it, her snout's a squashed slipper-face,
The mouth grin-long and perfunctory,
Undershot predatory. And the iris, dirty gold
Distilled only enough to be different
From the olive lode of her body,
The grained and woven blacks. And ringed larger
With a vaguer vision, an earlier eye
Behind her eye, paler, blinder,
Inward. Her buffalo hump
Begins the amazement of her progress.
Her mid-shoulder pectoral fin – concession
To fish-life – secretes itself
Flush with her concealing suit: under it
The skin's a pale exposure of deepest eel
As her belly is, a dulled pearl.
Strangest, the thumb-print skin, the rubberized weave
Of her insulation. Her whole body
Damascened with identity. This is she
Suspends the Sargasso
In her inmost hope. Her life is a cell
Sealed from event, her patience
Global and furthered with love
By the bending stars as if she
Were earth's sole initiate. Alone
In her millions, the moon's pilgrim,
The nun of water.

In the Dark Violin of the Valley

All night a music
Like a needle sewing body
And soul together, and sewing soul
And sky together and sky and earth
Together and sewing the river to the sea.

In the dark skull of the valley
A lancing, fathoming music
Searching the bones, engraving
On the glassy limits of ghost
In an entanglement of stars.

In the dark belly of the valley
A coming and going music
Cutting the bedrock deeper

To earth-nerve, a scalpel of music

The valley dark rapt
Hunched over its river, the night attentive
Bowed over its valley, the river

Crying a violin in a grave
All the dead singing in the river

The river throbbing, the river the aorta

And the hills unconscious with listening.

Strangers

Dawn. The river thins.
The combed-out coiffure at the pool-tail
Brightens thinly.
The slung pool's long hammock still flat out.

The sea-trout, a salt flotilla, at anchor,
Substanceless, flame-shadowed,
Hang in a near emptiness of sunlight.

There they actually are, under homebody oaks,
Close to teddybear sheep, near purple loosestrife –

Space-helms bowed in preoccupation,
Only a slight riffling of their tail-ailerons
Corrective of drift,
Gills easing.

And the pool's toiled rampart roots,
The cavorting of new heifers, water-skeeters
On their abacus, even the slow claim
Of the buzzard's hand
Merely decorate a heaven

Where the sea-trout, fixed and pouring,
Lean in the speed of light.
                              They make nothing
Of the hogweed sentry skeletons,
Nothing of the sun, so openly strafing down.

Thistle-floss bowls over them. First, lost leaves
Feel over them with unfeeling shadows.

The sea-trout, upstaring, in trance,
Absorb everything and forget it
Into a blank of bliss.

For this is the real Samadhi – worldless, levitated.

Till, bulging, a man-shape
Wobbles their firmament.
                              Now see the holy ones
Shrink their auras, slim, sink, focus, prepare
To scram like trout.

The Kingfisher

The Kingfisher perches. He studies.

Escaped from the jeweller's opium
X-rays the river's toppling
Tangle of glooms.

Now he's vanished – into vibrations.
A sudden electric wire, jarred rigid,
Snaps – with a blue flare.

He has left his needle buried in your ear.

Oafish oaks, kneeling, bend over
Dragging with their reflections
For the sunken stones. The Kingfisher
Erupts through the mirror, beak full of ingots,

And is away – cutting the one straight line
Of the raggle-taggle tumbledown river
With a diamond –

Leaves a rainbow splinter sticking in your eye.

Through him, God, whizzing in the sun,
Glimpses the angler.

Through him, God
Marries a pit
Of fishy mire.

        And look! He's
– gone again.
        Spark, sapphire, refracted
From beyond water
Shivering the spine of the river.

Visitation

All night the river's twists
Bit each other's tails, in happy play.

Suddenly a dark other
Twisted among them.

And a cry, half sky, half bird,
Slithered over roots.
             A star
Fleetingly etched it.

           Dawn
Puzzles a sunk branch under deep tremblings.

Nettles will not tell.
              Who shall say
That the river
Crawled out of the river, and whistled,
And was answered by another river?

A strange tree
Is the water of life –

Sheds these pad-clusters on mud-margins
One dawn in a year, her eeriest flower.

Performance

Just before the curtain falls in the river
The Damselfly, with offstage, inaudible shriek
Reappears, weightless.

Hover-poised, in her snake-skin leotards,
Her violet-dark elegance.

Eyelash-delicate, a dracula beauty,
In her acetylene jewels.

Her mascara smudged, her veils shimmer-fresh –

Late August. Some sycamore leaves
Already in their museum, eaten to lace.
Robin song bronze-touching the stillness
Over posthumous nettles. The swifts, as one,
Whipcracked, gone. Blackberries.
                      And now, lightly,
Adder-shock of this dainty assassin
Still in mid-passion –
                    still in her miracle play:
Masked, archaic, mute, insect mystery
Out of the sun's crypt.
                    Everything is forgiven
Such a metamorphosis in love!
Phaedra Titania
Dragon of crazed enamels!
Tragedienne of the ultra-violet,
So sulphurous and so frail,

Stepping so magnetically to her doom!

Lifted out of the river with tweezers
Dripping the sun's incandescence –

                          suddenly she
Switches her scene elsewhere.

        (Find him later, halfway up a nettle,
        A touch-crumple petal of web and dew –

        Midget puppet-clown, tranced on his strings,
        In the nightfall pall of balsam.)

Everything is on its Way to the River

*A near-sonnet, to assure Gavin Ewart that he isn't getting any
    older*

The bull — planting a tree — on its hind legs,
The dandelion clock — salvoes of dryness,
The elephants of granite — herds of slowness,
And the moonlighting hare with fleas in its lugs

Are on their way to the river.

With the stink-horn fungus' satyriasis,
The girl's blush that spills down over her breasts,
The hive's drunk legs — its bellyful of dark beasts,
The shivering favourite — lightning in its face.

The Lord's rainbow processions, in pomp, to the river.
Tombstone letters are wriggling lights on the river.
Continents are the hour-glass grains of the river.
All things draw to the river.
                                        Under them all
The river, itself and unalterable.

August Evening

Blue space burned out. Earth's bronzes cooling.
September
Edges this evening. Skyline trees hang charred.
The thistles
Survive a biological blaze – burnt splinters,
Skeletal carbons, crowned with ashes. The fuel
Nearly all gone.
                                And the river
Cools early, star-touched. New moon,
Not new leaf-curl tender, but crisp.
                                                        Mist
Breathes on the sliding glass. The river
Still beer-tinted from the barley disaster
Is becoming wintry.
                                The sea-tribes are here,
They've come up for their weddings, their Michaelmas fair,
The carnival on the gravels.
                                        Wet fog midnight,
A sheathing sea-freeze, hardens round my head,
Stiffens my fingers. Oaks and alders
Fume to black blots opposite.
The river lifts to a ghostly trail of smoke.

Too serious to stir, the longships
Of the sea-trout
Secretive under the land's levels,
Holds crammed with religious purpose,
Cobble the long pod of winter.
They will not play tonight.

Their procession kneels, in God-hush.
Robed in the stilled flow of their Creator
They inhale unending. I share it a little.

Slowly their white pathway sinks from the world.

The river becomes terrible.

Climbing out, I make a silent third
With two owls reassuring each other.

Last Night

The river seemed evil.
                    On the high fields, a full moon
Kept the world familiar. Moon-hazed
Hill over hill, the summer night
Turned on its pillow.
                    But down in the tree-cavern river,
The waded river, the river level with my knees,
The river under hangings of hemlock and nettle, and alder and
   oak,
Lay dark and grew darker. An evil mood
Darkened in it. Evil came up
Out of its stillest holes, and uncoiled
In the sick river, the drought river of slimes —
Like a sick man lying in the dark with his death.
Its darkness under roots, under old flood-battered boles
Was dark as blood,
Rusty peaty blood-dark, old-blood dark.
Something evil about the sunken river
In its sick-bed darkness. I stood in a grave
And felt the evil of fish. The strange evil
Of unknown fish-minds. Deep fish listening to me
In the dying river.

Eighty, and Still Fishing for Salmon

He holds
The loom of many rivers.
An old rowan now, arthritic, mossed,
Indifferent to man, roots for grave.

He's watching the Blackwater
Through hotel glass. Estuary nets
Empty. The river fishless. He's a trophy
Of the Great Days – his wrinkles, his tweeds,

And that armchair. And the Tussaud stillness.
Probably he's being tossed
Across a loch on Harris.
Both worlds have been lost

By the ritual mask
That hangs on its nail.
Soon he'll be out there, walking the sliding scree
Of the river – and over and over

His fly will come round on the vacant swirl.

An old Noh dancer, alone in the wind with his dance.
An air-fed, mountain prayer-wheel
Loyal to inbuilt bearings, touch of weather,
Though the heavens fail.

October Salmon

He's lying in poor water, a yard or so depth of poor safety,
Maybe only two feet under the no-protection of an outleaning
   small oak,
Half under a tangle of brambles.

After his two thousand miles, he rests,
Breathing in that lap of easy current
In his graveyard pool.

About six pounds weight,
Four years old at most, and hardly a winter at sea –
But already a veteran,
Already a death-patched hero. So quickly it's over!

So briefly he roamed the gallery of marvels!
Such sweet months, so richly embroidered into earth's beauty-
   dress,
Her life-robe –
Now worn out with her tirelessness, her insatiable quest,
Hangs in the flow, a frayed scarf –

An autumnal pod of his flower,
The mere hull of his prime, shrunk at shoulder and flank,

With the sea-going Aurora Borealis
Of his April power –
The primrose and violet of that first upfling in the estuary –
Ripened to muddy dregs,
The river reclaiming his sea-metals.

In the October light
He hangs there, patched with leper-cloths.

Death has already dressed him
In her clownish regimentals, her badges and decorations,
Mapping the completion of his service,
His face a ghoul-mask, a dinosaur of senility, and his whole
    body
A fungoid anemone of canker –

Can the caress of water ease him?
The flow will not let up for a minute.

What a change! from that covenant of polar light
To this shroud in a gutter!
What a death-in-life – to be his own spectre!
His living body become death's puppet,
Dolled by death in her crude paints and drapes
He haunts his own staring vigil
And suffers the subjection, and the dumbness,
And the humiliation of the role!

And that is how it is,
That is what is going on there, under the scrubby oak tree,
    hour after hour,
That is what the splendour of the sea has come down to,
And the eye of ravenous joy – king of infinite liberty
In the flashing expanse, the bloom of sea-life,

On the surge-ride of energy, weightless,
Body simply the armature of energy
In that earliest sea-freedom, the savage amazement of life,
The salt mouthful of actual existence
With strength like light –

Yet this was always with him. This was inscribed in his egg.
This chamber of horrors is also home.
He was probably hatched in this very pool.

And this was the only mother he ever had, this uneasy channel
    of minnows
Under the mill-wall, with bicycle wheels, car-tyres, bottles
And sunk sheets of corrugated iron.
People walking their dogs trail their evening shadows across
    him.
If boys see him they will try to kill him.

All this, too, is stitched into the torn richness,
The epic poise
That holds him so steady in his wounds, so loyal to his doom,
    so patient
In the machinery of heaven.

That Morning

We came where the salmon were so many
So steady, so spaced, so far-aimed
On their inner map, England could add

Only the sooty twilight of South Yorkshire
Hung with the drumming drift of Lancasters
Till the world had seemed capsizing slowly.

Solemn to stand there in the pollen light
Waist-deep in wild salmon swaying massed
As from the hand of God. There the body

Separated, golden and imperishable,
From its doubting thought – a spirit-beacon
Lit by the power of the salmon

That came on, came on, and kept on coming
As if we flew slowly, their formations
Lifting us toward some dazzle of blessing

One wrong thought might darken. As if the fallen
World and salmon were over. As if these
Were the imperishable fish

That had let the world pass away –

There, in a mauve light of drifted lupins,
They hung in the cupped hands of mountains

Made of tingling atoms. It had happened.
Then for a sign that we were where we were
Two gold bears came down and swam like men

Beside us. And dived like children.
And stood in deep water as on a throne
Eating pierced salmon off their talons.

So we found the end of our journey.

So we stood, alive in the river of light
Among the creatures of light, creatures of light.

Notes

Elmet is still the name on maps for a part of West Yorkshire that includes the deep valley of the upper Calder and its watershed of Pennine moorland. These poems confine themselves to the upper Calder and the territory roughly encircled by a line drawn through Halifax (on the east), Keighley (on the north-east), Colne (on the north-west), Burnley (on the west), and Littleborough (on the south-west): an 'island' straddling the Yorks–Lancs border, though mainly in Yorkshire, and centred, in my mind, on Heptonstall. Elmet was the last independent Celtic kingdom in England and originally stretched out over the vale of York. I imagine it shrank back into the gorge of the upper Calder under historic pressures, before the Celtic survivors were politically absorbed into England. But even into the seventeenth century this narrow cleft and its side-ginnels, under the glaciated moors, were still a 'badlands', a sanctuary for refugees from the law. Defoe hid in Halifax to escape his creditors. In those days Halifax was a small country town, and the main stronghold, further up the valley, was Heptonstall. An old rhyme takes note of one aspect of the early shift of power:

> Halifax is made of wax
>   Heptonstall of stone.
> Halifax has many pretty girls,
>   Heptonstall's got none.

Heptonstall is now a straggly hill-top hamlet.

Physically inhospitable, cut off to north and south by the high moorland, the insularity of the valley was in some ways almost complete, in others anything but. It formed a natural highway, the pass (just north of the M62) between the Scandinavian pressures of the North Sea and the Celtic pressures of the Irish Sea; between Mersey and Humber, this was the top of the tide, from both seas: where the wrack washed up and stayed. The results – alternating between pressurized stagnation and fermenting independence – can be read into the region's history. In the Civil War the valley militia formulated their refusal to obey any order from the King lacking the full consent of Parliament in a document that was incorporated into Jefferson's Declaration of Independence (one of his ancestors, the first Secretary for Virginia, came from the valley). The region's early prosperity was based on wool (the household industry had shaped architectural features in the old farms and cottages). So, when the time came, the spirit of the place was ready to take advantage of mass-production, and wherever water ran mills sprang up. By the end of the nineteenth century the Calder was called 'the hardest worked river in England'. The tributary known as Colden Water (the 'moor-water' in the poem titled 'Crown Point Pensioners') comes down a small side-valley as a tiny stream, easy to jump across in many places, yet at one time even this trickle was the lifeline for no fewer than fourteen mills (and up near the top of it, in the thirteenth century, the first fulling mill on record). The main valley, now shorn of its forest of chimneys (and of most of its mills), trying to adapt to tourism, prides itself on the title 'Cradle of the Industrial Revolution'. Following hard on these mills, as Jacob on Esau, the Chartist Movement sprang up in the same cradle.

This confined separateness, with its peculiar conditions and history, had its Darwinian effect on the natives. The most recent and obvious imprint on them was made by Wesley's Methodism, or rather by the local mutation of it. When Wesley first saw the place and preached here, before the mills, he called it 'the most beautiful valley in England'. But his antithesis went on – 'with the most barbarous people'. He was looking at it before that 'barbarous' population became his most fanatic enthusiasts. Which is to say, before they had registered the full impact of Parson Grimshaw – the hell-fire Methodist preacher of Haworth in the latter part of the eighteenth century. In Mrs Gaskell's *Life of Charlotte Brontë* there is a vivid and convincing (familiar) account of the community, the human type, that Grimshaw had to deal with. To judge by the shock-wave, which could still be felt, I think, well into this century, he struck the whole region 'like a planet'. There is a marvellously evocative re-creation of his life in Glyn Hughes's novel *Where I Used to Play on the Green* (1982). Grimshaw's unusual force seems to have alarmed even Wesley a little. To a degree, he changed the very landscape. His heavenly fire, straight out of Blake's *Prophetic Books*, shattered the terrain into biblical landmarks: quarries burst open like craters, and chapels – the bedrock transfigured – materialized standing in them. The crumpled map of horizons became a mirage of the Holy Land. Grimshaw imposed this vision (which was not a little neurotic), then herded the people into it.

The men who built the chapels were the same who were building the mills. They perfected the art of perching their towering, massive, stone, prison-like structures on drop-offs where now you would only just graze sheep. When the local regimes (and combined operation) of Industry and Religion started to collapse in the 1930s, this architecture emerged into spectacular desolation – a grim sort of beauty. Ruin followed swiftly, as the mills began to close, the chapels to empty, and the high farms under the moor-edge, along the spring line, were one by one abandoned. When I came to consciousness there, in the 1930s, the process was already far gone, though the communities seemed to be still intact, still entirely absorbed by the life of the factories – or by the slump. But you could not fail to realize that the cataclysm had happened: to the population (in the First World War, where a single bad ten minutes in no-man's-land could wipe out a street or even a village), to the industry (the shift to the East in textile manufacture), and to the Methodism (the new age). Gradually it dawned on you that you were living among the survivors, in the remains.

CAVE BIRDS

In this sequence, where the dramatis personae are the bird-spirits of people, or people with bird-spirits, each poem is designed as a masque-like tableau, to make an 'alchemical' ritual drama of transformation, with beginning, middle, end, and a good outcome.

RIVER

It is not easy to separate the fascination of rivers from the fascination of fish. Making dams, waterfalls, water-gardens, water-courses, is deeply absorbing play, for most of us, but the results have to be a home for something. When the water is wild, inhabitants are even more important. Streams, rivers, ponds, lakes *without fish* communicate to me one of the ultimate horrors – the poisoning of the wells, death at the source of all that is meant by water. I spent my first eight years beside the West Yorkshire River Calder – in which the only life was a teeming bankside population of brown rats. But the hillside streams and the canal held fish – including, in the canal, big but rare trout. These preoccupied me, as a lifeline might. Later on, in South Yorkshire, the farm which was for years my playground was bounded on one side by the River Don, which drained the industrial belt between Sheffield and Doncaster: a river of such concentrated steaming, foaming poisons that an accidental ducking was said to be fatal. My lifeline there was an old oxbow of the Don, full of fish and waterfowl. One day (early 1940s) I saw all the fish in this lake bobbing their mouths at the surface: the beginning of the end, as it turned out. That same day I noticed a strange ruddy vein in the ditch water that drained from the farm buildings, two or three hundred yards away. And I registered a new smell. I traced the vein to a big stone shed, packed with sodden, dark-stained grass – reeking the new smell. It was the first silage.

'Salmon-Taking Times' (page 126)

Atlantic Salmon dig nests, called 'redds', in the river gravel, covering their eggs with more gravel. In the British Isles, spawning begins in November, but might go on into January. After spawning, all the male fish die, as do some of the females – of exhaustion. The baby fish hatch in March, or thereabouts, and stay in the river, feeding on tiny organisms, for two, three, or even four years, depending on the feed and the individuality of the fish. When they get to five or six inches, one April or May these 'parr', as they are called, decide to go to sea, and begin to change colour. From looking very like brown trout they become silvery 'smolts', and instead of sticking each to its little territory and defending it fiercely, they drop downriver – into the estuary and eventually to sea, travelling in shoals. Where they go then depends on the feed, which depends in turn on changing factors of ocean currents, ocean temperatures. Some reappear after their first winter at sea, by which time they weigh five or six pounds. Others come back after two winters, weighing anything between eight pounds and twice that – or even more. The fish that stay out for three winters begin to be seriously big specimens, if they survive the thousand perils. Here and there, females will be returning to spawn for a second or even a third time.

Nature keeps all options open, so these fish begin to come back as early as February. In the days when nothing disturbed the cycle, smaller or larger shoals went on arriving through the year, entering the rivers and running up at times of high river flow. Each fish is programmed to return to the river, to the tributary, and even to the very pool, perhaps the very gravel patch, of its birth. Some make a mistake, but then might swim long distances to correct it. The moment they enter freshwater, they cease to feed, and so from that moment begin to lose condition, while the eggs or milt, which are small and undeveloped early in the year, begin to grow and ripen, cannibalizing the body-fat and muscle of the parent. In other words, with every day in the river, the salmon grows slightly less tasty. By the time eggs or milt are fully developed, and the moment for spawning arrives, the fish itself is inedible: all goodness has gone into eggs and milt, and the flesh is left whitish, flavourless, even disgusting. Smoked, or otherwise disguised, this is the salmon that country hotel guests often encounter in autumn and winter.

As spawning time approaches, the cock fish in particular go through a physical transformation: their colouring – reds and blacks – can become almost violent, like warpaint. At the same time, their heads and especially their jaws change, the tip of their underjaw hooks up in a 'kipe', sometimes grotesque, like a rhino horn on the chin instead of the nose-end. Meanwhile, if they have been in the river some months, many will have developed patches of fungus – if not the full-blown Ulcerative Dermal Necrosis (that hit rivers in the British Isles at the end of the 1960s, and has all but wiped out some stocks).

Since salmon do not feed in freshwater (though they will catch and crush flies in their mouths, and suck worms), they have to find easy ways of saving energy throughout their wait for November. The favoured solution is to lie as if in coma, inaccessibly preoccupied, immune to any temptation. But for every salmon (at least, this is the faith) there is a time of the day – perhaps only a few minutes – when the fish is alert, active, craving to do something. At this moment they can sometimes be caught. Some experts maintain that the moment coincides with a certain phase in the constantly changing availability of oxygen in the water. It is recognizable externally by an atmospheric feeling, to which birds, insects and animals (and human beings) also seem to respond.

'The Bear' (page 138)
Most of this book was prompted by observations made on rivers in the British Isles. 'The Bear' is a memory of the Dean River, in British Columbia. Steelhead are rainbow trout, born in the river (like salmon), but going to sea and returning (like salmon and the size of salmon) to spawn where they were born. They are an immensely powerful and glamorous fish, with a mystique of their own: the great prize of the Pacific North-West. My three companions, fanatic 'steelheaders', two Canadians and one American, would never dream of killing one of these creatures. 'If we killed them,' they say, 'we'd be like you people in England: we wouldn't have any.'

'That Morning' (page 178)
The river in 'That Morning', like the Gulkana, is in Alaska. King Salmon is the Alaskan name for the Chinook – the biggest of the five species of Pacific salmon. All Pacific salmon die after spawning. The 'drift of Lancasters' is simply a memory of South Yorkshire from a late phase of the Second World War. On many evenings, for the last two hours of daylight (then on into darkness), the whole sky would be full of four-engined bombers, from airfields further north, on their way to the great raids. For those hours everything, the whole landscape, would be gripped by that drumming – a different sensation from sitting in cellars listening to the curious, inside-the-head throbbing of Dorniers, as they crept up the line of the River Don to bomb Sheffield, night after night a few years earlier.